WHOLE-GRAIN MORNINGS

WITHDRAWN

Whole-Grain MORNINGS

New Breakfast Recipes to Span the Seasons

Megan Gordon

Photography by Clare Barboza

TEN SPEED PRESS
Berkeley

Published in the United States by Ten Speed Press, an imprint of the Crown Publishing Group,
a division of Random House LLC, New York, a Penguin Random House Company.
www.crownpublishing.com
www.tenspeed.com

Ten Speed Press and the Ten Speed Press colophon are
registered trademarks of Random House LLC.

All photographs by Clare Barboza with the exception of photographs on pages
vi, 6, 8, 9, 39, 41, 45, 46, 49, 53, 59, 66, 69, 70, 74, 77, 85, 99, 100, 102, 105, 108, 115,
125, 127, 135, 136, 139, 142, 165, 168, 171 which are by the author.

Library of Congress Cataloging-in-Publication Data

Gordon, Megan, 1979-
  Whole-grain mornings : new breakfast recipes to span the seasons / Megan Gordon.
    pages cm
1. Breakfasts 2. Cooking (Cereals) 3. Grain. I. Title.
  TX733.G66 2013
  641.3'31—dc23
                          2013015594

Hardcover ISBN: 978-1-60774-500-6
eBook ISBN: 978-1-60774-501-3

Printed in China

Design by Sarah Adelman
Food styling by Julie Hopper

10 9 8 7 6 5 4 3 2 1

First Edition

Contents

to MY MOM AND DAD,
with immense gratitude.

to SAM,
with my whole heart.

BEGINNINGS

I LEARNED TO COOK BY OBSERVATION AND TRIAL AND ERROR. As a girl, I'd sit on the counter while my mom made dinner, feet dangling, snacking on Cheerios. On nights when we'd have lasagna, she would reserve the broken shards of cooked noodles and I'd form small ricotta roll-ups to busy myself. I'd lay them out in neat rows, smitten with my own productivity. A few years later, I realized that a whole pan of lasagna was really just ricotta roll-ups on a larger scale: an act of repetition with noodles, sauce, and cheese. Soon I was making my own lasagna with very minimal assistance—beaming with pride the whole way through.

On Sunday evenings after putting my sisters and me to bed, my mom would write out what we'd have for dinner that week as a way to organize her weekly trips to the grocery store. The sheet of yellow legal paper was always taped to the refrigerator, so when we'd pass by the kitchen Monday morning, excitement grew as we thought about our favorite upcoming meal. Generally it was simple food that could be tackled after a long day of teaching, with small kids underfoot: spaghetti and meatballs, turkey potpie, tuna casserole, or baked chicken. Our meals never looked like those picture-perfect moments of dinner that we'd see on television, with everyone digging in and sharing the details of their day. Instead, that hour was filled with three picky girls (or later, moody teenagers) and tired, overworked parents. But we always showed up nonetheless. In our house dinnertime was a statement that cooking and eating together at the same table was important. It was family.

Much like my mom, my grandmother is a gracious home cook. She makes a mean coconut cake with seven-minute frosting and her Jell-O salad is enthusiastically requested at holidays and reunions. My other grandmother, my dad's mom, also tended toward simple recipes. From each of them, it wasn't noteworthy dishes or standout techniques that were passed down, so much as an appreciation and affinity for practice, repetition, and tradition. And so today I call myself a home cook, too. There's a certain pride in the term that itself seems passed down by generations of women who learned by watching their mothers, reading cookbooks, paying attention, and pulling up a seat at the table. By dabbling and then diving in. So here we are.

ABOUT THIS BOOK

I've always wanted to write a breakfast book. It's the meal we all start with, the meal that ushers us into the day. Even more, I wanted to write a book that reflects the way I do breakfast, acknowledging the fact that what we eat looks different on a cold, gray morning in February than it does on a sunny morning in June. A busy Wednesday brings about different breakfast options than does a leisurely Sunday. Sure, some of that has to do with the available produce. But a lot of it has to do with what we're drawn to in those different months or what our bodies crave. So I decided to split this book into seasonal chapters and further divide each chapter, noting which recipes are best for busy weekdays, slow Sundays, or brunch. I hope you return to the book as the months pass, the seasons change, and friends and family trickle in and out to join you at the breakfast table throughout the year.

In addition to a seasonal breakfast book, I wanted to write a somewhat personal book, beginning in the San Francisco Bay Area and ending in Seattle. A book that tracks a particular season in my life, as much as the many breakfasts from that time—the story of a high school English teacher searching for a new school and landing in a bakery instead. The story of that accidental baker waking before sunrise to crimp pies and bake granola, finding herself looking at the work of a graphic designer one thousand miles away who might be able to help with branding the business.

That story is obviously mine. And that designer, Sam? It's now his, too. Sam worked for me for a little less than a year as I began my baking business, Marge. During this time, we met once face-to-face at a little café in the Fremont neighborhood of Seattle, discussing websites and logos and drinking spicy chai. As was often the case, we fell into our usual digressions about folk music, films we liked, and good cheese. When our client relationship had come to an end, we threw ourselves into much longer phone calls, letters, travels across several states, and more than a few breakfasts together. Then, after too many seasons apart, Sam flew down to help me load a large U-Haul and make the long drive up the coast from San Francisco to a new home in Seattle. Today we share a bright blue craftsman house, a modest garden, and a very large comingled collection of books. While a good handful of the recipes in this cookbook were originally written in my shoebox kitchen in Northern California, many grew naturally from our new life here in Seattle. I think they might travel just as easily to your kitchen, too, regardless of where that may be.

ABOUT THE RECIPES

While this is technically a whole-grain cookbook, I don't consider it a "health book" or a definitive reference on whole-grain cooking. Within these pages, you'll find cheese and butter and even a little bacon. But each recipe features whole grains as the star because they're a nourishing way to start the morning, and I've relied on them as such for years. I gravitate toward savory recipes more and more these days, so you'll see breakfast ideas here that you might not normally think of as morning fare. My ultimate goal in writing these recipes is that you'll stumble across something you're inspired to make in your own kitchen.

Big picture aside, there are a few things to know about the way I've structured the chapters and recipes. First, each chapter will open with a brief introduction that includes a **Seasonal Spotlight**, featuring different fruits and vegetables that I cook with during those months and a few quick tips about selecting, storing, and preparing them. Then each recipe is slotted into a section: **Busy Weekdays**, **Slow Sundays**, or **Brunch**, based on the amount of time and effort it takes or **Spreads and Toppings** for accompaniments. Within most recipes, you'll see a few lines I call **Morning Notes**, where I include additional information on ingredients or preparation—good things to know before getting started. At the end of each recipe, you may see a few lines I call **Make Ahead**, which will address how to maximize your time, and **Make It Your Own**, which will encourage you to adapt and experiment according to your tastes and preferences.

COOK'S NOTES

Measurements: I wrote this book using standard cup measurements, weight measurements in grams for baking ingredients and grains, and liquid measurements in milliliters. For fruits and vegetables, I list them as you'd buy them at the market, usually by the pound. In my experience, grams are used more often than ounces in baking recipes, and I have a baking background, so this is where I'm most comfortable. I like to weigh out my whole-grain flours and grains because amounts will always be accurate this way. One cup of barley flour, for example, can come in weighing more than another cup of barley flour depending on the brand, batch, or age, so if you use cup measurements alone, your results may vary—especially for more precise baking recipes. All that being said, use whichever measurement (standard cups or grams) you're most apt to cook with eagerly and confidently.

Cooking times: Much like with measurements, whole-grain cooking times can vary noticeably depending on the age of the grains and the company you buy them from. So get into something of a Zen headspace when you're setting out to cook your grains, knowing it may take more time (or even less time) than you'd anticipated. While I give standard time suggestions on the chart on page 22, if you're buying packaged specialty grains, do follow the instructions given by the producer. They know more about their product than any chart that aims to be universal. Last, within each recipe, the oven times are based on my standard electric home oven. I recommend getting an oven thermometer so we can all hope to be on the same page. But even so, know that different ovens have their own quirks, so spend a little time getting to know the hot spots in your own.

Nitty gritty: In some of the recipes you'll find in this book, I call for *cooked* grains (see Cooking Whole Grains, page 20). If a recipe asks that you cook your grains in a different liquid or toast them first, I don't specify "cooked" and instead walk you through the preparation. I like precooking a big batch of grains so I don't have to think about waking up early to do so in the morning—and this is the idea behind most of the recipes you'll find in the Busy Weekdays category of each season. Each of those recipes can be conquered in under an hour (and often downright fast) although this often assumes you'll cook the grains in advance.

MY COOKING STYLE, YOUR COOKING STYLE

We're all drawn to the kitchen for different reasons, and we're each a different kind of cook. I tend to be a big planner and measurer, not as confident flying by the seat of my pants without written notes and already thought-through ideas. But after years and years of following other people's recipes, I've also gotten good at developing my own based on how I like to eat at home. My cooking style tends to be quite simple: leftover grains, chopped herbs from the garden, and a poached egg satisfy me completely. I don't fear fat. I eat eggs, drink whole milk, and eat full-fat yogurt. I do, however, really limit sugar because it leaves me feeling tired and down. I've made a switch to using mostly natural sugars at home, and you'll see that reflected in the recipes here. So that's me. But we're all different. Thank goodness.

During my years as an English teacher, I'd always tell writing students to start thinking about their style before they took pen to paper. Looking back, it was a silly directive. You can't find your style until you start writing. A lot. And you can't find your style in the kitchen until you start spending time there. The more you're in the kitchen, the pieces will slowly click and you'll realize what ingredients you're drawn to and what excites you. It's my sincere hope that you work these recipes into *your own* cooking style, taking from them what's useful and leaving the rest behind. All the while, hopefully not taking yourself too seriously. After all, while it is the most important meal of the day, it is still just breakfast. When you fumble, there's a chance to do it all over again the next morning.

No.9287:Millet

No.W29c: Quinoa

THE PANTRY

THIS SECTION GIVES YOU A PEEK INTO MY CUPBOARDS and a few of the ingredients I use most often throughout the week. You may well have many of these on hand in your own kitchen, and those you don't should be relatively easy to track down. For information on where I buy ingredients outside of Seattle or online, see Sources, page 166.

FRUITS

I frequently use seasonal fruit in morning dishes and desserts. In each recipe, I'll indicate when you can use fresh or frozen (usually you can choose either), but I do recommend finding local fresh fruit whenever you can. While I aim to buy organic fruits and produce, I will often choose peaches or apples from a local farmer at the market that may not be organic rather than peaches or apples that have traveled far and wide but happen to be certified. I do always opt for organic fruit for zesting as the rind is the last stop for many of the chemicals used in the spraying of nonorganic citrus fruits.

SALTS, SPICES, AND HERBS

In personality, I'm very much a baker in the sense that I like to measure out ingredients precisely and don't often stray from those measurements. But the more I watch intuitive cooks who work utterly without recipes, the more inspired I am to step out on a limb with a laid-back approach. I've gotten much better about trusting my instincts and intuition when it comes to seasoning the food I make at home and, in doing so, have come to rely on a small arsenal of spices and herbs.

Kosher salt: The recipes in this book have been tested with Diamond Crystal kosher salt. Kosher salt has larger granules than fine-grain table or sea salt, so it takes up more volume (and therefore, pound for pound, will come across as less salty). If you're using a more common table or sea salt, adjust accordingly: scale back about 50 percent of the

recommended amount of kosher salt. So if a recipe calls for 1 teaspoon kosher salt, you should start with ½ teaspoon fine table salt and adjust from there as needed.

Flaky finishing salt: I use a coarse finishing salt like Maldon to sprinkle on top of savory dishes, eggs, warm cereals, oatmeal, and porridge.

Spices: To get the most flavor from your spices, consider grinding them yourself. I try to avoid those little glass spice jars at the supermarket and aim to buy in bulk instead. (You can never tell how long those jars have been sitting on store shelves, losing flavor each month that passes.) The spices I use most often are cinnamon, cardamom, ginger, nutmeg, coriander, cumin, a good curry powder, cayenne pepper, and red pepper flakes.

Herbs: I love using fresh herbs whenever possible and am constantly trying, with each passing season, to become a better gardener. A few herbs I reach for most often are thyme, rosemary, sage, chives, dill, and parsley. For truer flavor, it's always best to use fresh herbs if you can, and that's what I call for often in this book. If they're not available or you'd prefer to use dried herbs, a good rule of thumb is to substitute dried herbs for fresh herbs at a ratio of 1 to 3. So if a recipe calls for 1 tablespoon fresh thyme, you'd use 1 teaspoon dried thyme instead.

OILS AND FATS

I feel more satisfied throughout the day if I have a little fat and protein for breakfast. I look for organic, unrefined oils that have been as minimally processed as possible, and I make sure to store them in a cool spot to keep them from going rancid.

Extra-virgin olive oil: Cold-pressed extra-virgin olive oil gets daily play in my kitchen. It comes from the first pressing of the olives, which produces a higher-quality oil with less acidity, and it's easy to track down in most grocery stores. Olive oils have distinct flavor differences: some are quite grassy, while others are fruity or smooth. For this reason, I stock a few different kinds: an herbal, higher-end oil that I save for salad dressings and finishing dishes, and an all-purpose bottle for general use and baking.

Organic unrefined coconut oil: You can find this naturally saturated fat in glass jars at the grocery store. It's solid at room temperature, stable at higher temperatures, subtly sweet, and mildly fragrant. If you specifically look for virgin coconut oil, you're getting a wonderfully unprocessed product. If a jar of coconut oil doesn't indicate that it's virgin, it's likely highly processed. At the time of printing this book, Trader Joe's sells a fantastic, inexpensive organic virgin coconut oil.

Unsalted butter: I always bake with unsalted butter because it allows more control over the salt in any given recipe. When I lived in San Francisco, I was lucky to find Straus Creamery butter, an übercreamy, rich butter. In Seattle it's trickier to find Straus, so I look for any good, organic European-style butter to spread on crusty bread with a sprinkle of flaky salt, or to add to my warm porridge in the morning.

Safflower oil: Flavorless and colorless with a high smoke point, this a good oil to reach for if you're frying foods or cooking them at very high heat. I use organic cold expeller-pressed safflower oil, but you could certainly use a more standard neutral-flavored vegetable oil like canola oil as well.

NATURAL SWEETENERS

Sugar certainly has its place in many baking and cooking recipes, but when it's used too often or too liberally, you're left with quick-burning energy that's gone in no time. That said, tart berries or rhubarb need a dash of sugar to soften them into a velvety sauce or chunky jam, and oatmeal is wonderful with a generous dollop of maple syrup or honey. So I don't shy away from sugar altogether or aim to cook sugar-free, but I do use natural sweeteners whenever possible. Here are a few you'll see most often in this book.

Brown rice syrup: This natural sweetener is half as sweet as white sugar and has a mild, almost caramel flavor. Made with brown rice that's been cultured and then cooked down to a syrup, its thick personality makes it a clear choice for recipes that need a little binding, like the Trail Guide Nut and Seed Bars (page 146). It's nice in coffee and tea, too.

Honey: Robert MacKimmie, owner of the San Francisco–based honey business City Bees, harvests honey from different neighborhoods all around the city. Honey from one hive tastes (and looks!) quite different from a batch harvested across town. Robert taught me a lot about the way the flavor varies and the importance of buying local honey when you can (many folks believe that eating local honey helps your body adjust to seasonal changes and can even prevent allergies). I try to find raw, unprocessed honey because the heat used in processing more commercial honeys can kill many of the good enzymes and minerals.

Maple syrup: This liquid sweetener is made from the boiled sap of sugar maple trees and is sold in varying grades. Grade A is the lightest and, in my opinion, is great for pancakes but a bit too mild for baking. Grade B is the syrup you want for baking or cooking. It has a stronger, more complex flavor. Regardless of grade, try to find organic syrup to avoid chemicals that are occasionally used when straining out the syrup from the tap. Also, it's a good idea to refrigerate your syrup once open to prolong shelf life.

Molasses: With its characteristic dark flavor, this thick natural sweetener is made from boiling sugarcane. It contains more simple sugars than honey or cane sugar, so it absorbs slowly and steadily in the body. I usually buy unsulfured blackstrap molasses because it comes from the final press of sugarcane and contains lots of great minerals and iron.

Natural cane sugar: Many of the recipes in this book call for natural cane sugar, a class of sweeteners made from sugarcane that's been crushed to extract its juice. They're only minimally processed and haven't been stripped of their vitamins and minerals like more conventional sugars. Each one has a slightly different flavor, so instead of just reaching for a substance to generally sweeten a dish, you can begin to think about the subtlety each would impart. The three I use most often are demerara, turbinado, and muscavodo sugars. Demerara and turbinado sugars are amber-hued with coarser granules than processed white or brown sugar. Muscovado sugar is an unrefined, unbleached sugar with a much darker flavor and a delightfully moist, almost sticky texture. It gives a nice chew and a rich, distinct flavor to baked goods. All are easy to find at most of the grocery stores in Seattle, but if you have trouble at your home market, see Sources, page 166, for a good online retailer.

DAIRY

Many of the recipes in this book call for milk or yogurt. I buy whole milk and whole-milk yogurt (when I'm not making my own) because I prefer the taste, but in most cases you can use low-fat or nonfat dairy if you'd prefer. In recipes where I advise using whole milk specifically for a more successful end product, I will let you know in the ingredients list. Likewise, I'll often give recommendations for my favorite type of yogurt for a certain recipe—sometimes Greek yogurt is more appropriate than runny, European-style yogurt, and vice versa.

NUTS AND SEEDS

Many recipes in this book call for toasted nuts either as a main ingredient or as a garnish of sorts. You will also see a lot of seeds in these recipes too. From granolas to energy bars, they play a big role in how I do breakfast. In most cases, the recipes are adaptable, so feel free to swap in your favorite nuts and seeds. For a long list of candidates, see Toppings and Stir-Ins, page 44. Note: When you see "pepitas" listed in a recipe, do know that I am referring to the delightfully crunchy green pumpkin seeds that are easy to find in most bulk bins.

Toasting nuts is a wonderful way to draw out their natural sweet flavors and tone down any inherent bitterness. I find myself reaching for nuts often because they're a great source of fiber, omega-3 fatty acids, and unsaturated fats. I sprinkle toasted nuts on morning oats, the tops of muffins, and warm grain bowls alike. Paired with a spoonful of thick honey, they make even the most humble bowl of plain yogurt sing.

If you want to ensure you're working with the freshest nuts, it's best to buy them raw and toast them yourself as they go rancid much more quickly once they've been toasted. Plus, a lot of toasted nuts you buy from the store have unnecessary added salt and oil. So while it does add a few extra minutes to a recipe, toasting your own is well worth the time. My one exception is that I buy toasted and skinned hazelnuts from a great farm in Oregon that grows, roasts, and skins their own (see Sources, page 167).

Storing Nuts

Because I like to see them, I store nuts in glass jars in my pantry out of any direct sunlight. I use them relatively quickly, so I don't worry about them going rancid. However, you can refrigerate most raw nuts for up to 3 months or freeze them for up to 6 months.

Chopping Nuts

Toasting nuts draws out their natural oils, so while it seems like a fussy detail, I wait until they've cooled completely to chop them. Most of the recipes in this book call for coarsely chopped nuts, so I never use the food processor, relying on a good kitchen knife and a steady hand instead.

Toasting Nuts

Because toasted nuts go rancid even more quickly than raw nuts, I generally only toast them as I need them. On the following page, I provide instructions for toasting different kinds of nuts in the oven. If you can't be bothered with preheating the oven—especially for a small batch of nuts—you can toast them in a hot, dry skillet on the stovetop instead. You want to cook them just until fragrant over medium heat. Know that they can go from raw to burned relatively quickly, so jiggle and shake your pan as you go. Once toasted, transfer the nuts to a dry plate to cool before chopping or using.

Toasting times: I toast all raw nuts at 350°F on a rimmed baking sheet. Do note that the times below can vary a bit depending on the variety of nut and whether they're whole, sliced, or chopped.

- Whole almonds: 7 to 8 minutes
- Slivered or sliced almonds: 5 to 6 minutes
- Pepitas: 5 to 7 minutes
- Pecans: 7 to 10 minutes
- Walnuts: 8 to 9 minutes

Hazelnuts: When you buy hazelnuts at the store, they have a thin, dark skin on them that is perfectly fine to eat, but many recipes will ask that you remove the skins because they can impart a slightly bitter flavor and their texture is often undesired. You can purchase hazelnuts that have already been toasted and skinned (see Sources, page 167), but to do so yourself is simple: Place the hazelnuts on a small baking sheet. Toast for 10 to 12 minutes. Remove from the oven and scoop immediately onto a clean kitchen towel. Fold up the towel so the nuts are completely covered, and use a quick back-and-forth motion to create friction inside the towel and ease the skins off. Repeat as necessary. Don't aim for perfection here—getting the majority of the skins removed is usually just fine.

Sesame seeds: Hulled sesame seeds are very white or light yellow (they have the outer shell removed). They toast relatively quickly (4 to 5 minutes), whereas seeds with hulls intact still have their light brown outer shell and take longer to toast (8 to 9 minutes).

WHOLE-GRAIN FLOURS

I grew up on white flour and baked with it throughout most of my teenage and college years. But I traveled more and more in my late twenties and early thirties, and my favorite way to get to know a new city and its neighborhoods is to visit its bakeries. Whether on the streets of Taos, New Mexico, or the narrow alleys of Quito, Ecuador, I found myself gravitating toward baked goods made with whole-grain flours. They felt more substantial and fulfilled me in a way that sweets made with white flour did not. Many years ago, I started working more with whole-grain flours in my own kitchen, and I've included a few that I use most here. If you have gluten sensitivities, I've indicated (GF) below for flours that are naturally gluten-free.

While experimenting with whole-grain flours is always encouraged, be aware that their gluten and protein levels differ greatly, so just doing a simple swap in a recipe doesn't always work. To begin using whole-grain flours instead of white flour, you could start out by swapping one-fourth to half the amount of all-purpose flour in a recipe with a whole-grain flour of your choosing and take it from there. It's always an experiment, and you learn as you go. The tweaking becomes endless and, hopefully, enjoyable.

White whole wheat flour: I often turn to King Arthur brand white whole wheat flour instead of regular whole wheat flour. It's milled from hard white spring wheat instead of traditional red wheat, so it results in baked goods with a lighter color and gentler texture. You can substitute this for 100 percent of the all-purpose flour in many baking recipes.

Whole wheat pastry flour: Much lighter than a typical whole wheat flour, whole wheat pastry flour has a special lightness thanks to the lower protein and gluten content. It's used most often when you want a more delicate crumb, so it's great in muffin or quick bread recipes.

Barley flour: Barley flour has a subtle sweetness that makes it perfect for morning recipes and an easy choice when baking with fruit. I'll often substitute barley flour for half of the all-purpose flour called for in a recipe (avoid the temptation to use all barley flour as it's very low in gluten, so you'll have mighty flat scones or biscuits).

Oat flour (GF): This increasingly common flour is pale in color and faintly sweet in flavor. I'm fond of using it when baking with berries or chocolate. To make your own oat flour, simply pulse rolled oats in a food processor until they turn to a fine powder.

Spelt: If you want to start experimenting right away with a whole-grain flour other than standard whole wheat flour, you should scribble spelt flour onto your grocery list. It acts much like an all-purpose white flour in baking recipes and has a neutral flavor and color.

Buckwheat flour (GF): This flour stands out both in appearance and flavor. Its grayish purple color and velvety texture make it a real stunner, and its assertive, forward flavor has bold fruity notes, so it pairs really well with heartier fall fruits like apples and pears. I find myself reaching for it often in the cooler months to make pancakes, waffles, and crepes.

EQUIPMENT

A cook's tools are important. But I've never been one to stock the kitchen with gadgets and appliances, and I certainly wouldn't feel comfortable advocating that you should. However, there are some good stand-bys that will help you make your way through the recipes in this book, and hopefully you either already have them at home or know a friendly neighbor who does.

Pans, skillets, and such: When I refer to a *large pan* or skillet in a recipe, I'm indicating that a 12-inch pan would be best. For a *medium pan* or skillet, a 10-inch pan is ideal. A *cast-iron skillet* is my go-to for dishes that are cooked on the stovetop and then baked further in the oven. They come in a variety of sizes and are great for cooking everything from bacon to apple crisp. A *nonstick pan* is nice for eggs, crepes, and pancakes. I own a few sizes of Pyrex *baking dishes*: an 8 by 8-inch, 11 by 7-inch, and 9 by 13-inch. A trusty *rimmed baking sheet* to toast nuts and make breakfast cookies is a must (18 by 13-inch half sheet pans are versatile and ever useful). To cook your grains, you'll need a *2-quart stainless steel pot* that will distribute heat evenly (to prevent grains from sticking) or a *Dutch oven* with a tight-fitting lid for larger batches of grains.

Thermometers and scales: To make homemade yogurt, you will need a *candy thermometer*. I have an inexpensive digital one, but a more traditional candy thermometer will work just fine, too. A *kitchen scale* is always handy, especially when weighing out whole-grain flours (if you decide to use gram measurements instead of standard cups). Last, I do recommend getting a little *oven thermometer* to verify that the read on your oven is, in fact, accurate. You can find them for around five dollars.

Kitchen utensils and tools: I think every kitchen needs a good *whisk*, a *chef's knife* with an 8- to 10-inch blade for tasks like chopping onions, and a *paring knife* with a 4- to 5-inch blade for cutting and coring fruits and vegetables. A few *wooden spoons* are good for stirring batters, a *heatproof spatula* will help flip pancakes and frittatas, and *tongs* are great for removing bacon from a pan. I love my *box grater* because I can choose different size holes depending on my purpose (large for potatoes, very small for Parmesan). A *Microplane grater* is most helpful for citrus zest, and a *vegetable peeler* is an inexpensive must for peeling carrots, potatoes, and the like.

Appliances: You will need a *blender* and a *food processor* for a few of the recipes in this book. I use my food processor all the time for making everything from homemade bread crumbs to herby pesto. If you were to splurge on one new kitchen item, I love my *yogurt maker* (I have an older Euro Cuisine model). If you eat yogurt even a few times a week, it'll pay for itself in no time.

Etcetera: I find *parchment paper* infinitely useful in the kitchen to avoid having baked goods stick to baking sheets. *Cheesecloth* is a must for making homemade almond milk and hazelnut milk and is nice to have around to strain yogurts or puddings. I use a *wire-mesh colander* to rinse vegetables and a *fine-weave colander* to rinse grains. A *spice grinder* will help you to grind fresh spices; I use an old coffee grinder that's designated just for spices. Last, a trusty *cutting board* is an essential for prepping and chopping.

WHY WHOLE GRAINS?

Whole grains are packed with fiber, protein, and amino acids. They give you ample energy and satisfy until your next meal. But truthfully, that's not the main reason I'm drawn to whole grains. They've become a cornerstone of my cooking because they're so simple to form a meal around and each grain has its own distinct flavor, so things rarely get boring or dull. While I often make whole grains the center of a meal, they can also be a convenient vessel for jammy fruits, a poached egg, sautéed seasonal vegetables, creamy yogurt, and crunchy toppings. In this way, they are my empty slate in the morning—how I prepare them and what I add to them changes with the seasons or my mood or what I have on hand. But it almost always comes back to grains.

When many people think about whole grains, they remember days of veggie loaf in college cafeterias or dense and inedible slices of dark bread. Thankfully, things have changed. In this book you'll find warm buckwheat crepes with rich sautéed plums, and creamy rice cereal with honey-poached figs. You'll find toothsome oats with a glug of cream, and farmers' market berries folded gently into cornmeal custard. Each recipe is a far cry from the lifeless, hard-as-a-rock whole-grain foods that you may remember from hippie grocery stores, rigid cookbooks, or health-conscious aunts (we all have one, yes?) in the eighties and beyond. You won't find those here.

WHAT EXACTLY IS A WHOLE GRAIN?

Whole grains are actually seeds that have a high percentage of protein, fiber, vitamins, and complex carbohydrates. They contain three edible parts: the bran (the coating that protects the grain and the source of most of the fiber), the germ (nestled right inside the endosperm, it's the nutrient powerhouse of the grain), and the endosperm, the largest part of the grain but also the starchiest. The nutrient-poor, carbohydrate-rich endosperm contains the smallest amounts of vitamins and minerals; it's what you have left when the bran and the germ are stripped away in the refining process. So you can see that if you're buying refined grains, flours, and breads, you're missing out on most of the nutrients inherent in whole grains.

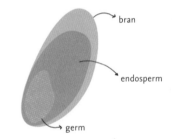

BUYING AND STORING WHOLE GRAINS

Unless I'm ordering specialty grains online, I almost always buy my grains from the bulk bins at the grocery store. If you're shopping at a store with a relatively high turnover, this will ensure they're much fresher than packages that have been sitting on shelves for a long time. It's also usually cheaper and allows you to experiment, trying just a handful of grains that may be new to you without making a major commitment.

I store my grains in glass containers because I like to see them. If you'd prefer a different vessel, just be sure that it's airtight, and store them in a relatively cool spot in the house. Because whole grains contain natural oils, they can go rancid faster than you may think. As a very general rule, you should aim to use your whole grains within 3 months of purchasing them or store them in the refrigerator for up to 6 months.

RINSING AND SOAKING WHOLE GRAINS

Many folks like to rinse their grains to remove any possible dirt or grit, but I don't often find this necessary. The one exception is quinoa. While many times the naturally occurring (but bitter-tasting) saponin coating is removed from the quinoa you buy at the store, I rinse it just to be sure. Do note that you only want to rinse the grains you're going to cook for the recipe at hand. Grains can mold, so don't rinse the whole batch right away. To rinse, cover the grains with cold water in a large pot and drain using a fine-weave colander until the water runs clear.

As for soaking, many people believe soaking grains cuts down on cooking time and can even help them cook more evenly. I haven't found this to be true enough to warrant the forethought, so I rarely do it. An exception would be occasionally soaking steel-cut oats overnight to have a quicker oatmeal in the morning, or soaking barley for at least 1 hour and up to overnight, which does speed up its otherwise slow cooking time. If you do soak your grains overnight, they'll likely require about $^1/_4$ cup less cooking liquid per 1 cup of grains, so plan accordingly.

STORING, FREEZING, AND USING LEFTOVER GRAINS

If refrigerated and stored in an airtight container, most cooked grains should remain good for 4 to 5 days. Because grains tend to continue to soak up moisture after they're cooked, to reheat them you'll have to add extra liquid (water, milk, or nut milk) to loosen them up a bit. If you know you won't use your cooked and cooled grains in a few days, you can freeze them in sealable plastic bags for up to 3 months. Note that not all grains freeze equally well: heartier grains (rye berries, wheat berries, farro) freeze wonderfully, while tiny grains like amaranth do not. To thaw and reheat, place the grains and a few tablespoons of water in a saucepan over medium heat, cover, and cook until warmed through. If need be, drain away any excess water. You can also use the microwave if you prefer.

A DOZEN FAVORITE WHOLE GRAINS

Below you'll find twelve of my favorite morning grains. I've noted (GF) after each gluten-free grain in case that's a health concern for you, and I've divided the grains into two categories: quick cooking and slow cooking, so you can select your grains depending on how much time you have on any given morning. Additionally, you can get to know the grains in clusters based on cooking time, which is helpful if you want to swap one for another.

Some of the whole grains listed below are sold in very quick-cooking flake form (barley flakes, rye flakes, and spelt flakes, for example). Rolled grains, or grain flakes, are manufactured by steaming whole grains and pressing them to make flakes that you can use in recipes like oatmeal, muesli, and granola. They're fun to experiment with as each has a distinct flavor and texture (I particularly love rye flakes for their darker color and nutty flavor). You won't see specific cooking instructions for all the rolled grains in the Cooking Chart on page 22, but most cook in under 15 minutes, and the recipes in this book will guide you toward the correct preparation.

Quick Cooking

Most of the quick-cooking grains cook in 20 minutes or less.

Amaranth (GF): Often called a pseudograin, amaranth is actually the tiny seed of an herb. A true nutritional powerhouse, it's a great source of complete protein and contains lysine, an essential amino acid not often found in grains that helps with the absorption of calcium and bone growth. I almost always toast amaranth before cooking it—otherwise it can easily become the consistency of porridge (great when you're going for porridge; not so great when you're not). Some find the flavor of amaranth a bit grassy, so if you're new to the grain, start by pairing it with bold flavors like jammy fruits. I love popping it in a dry pan for 3 to 5 minutes for a simple, crunchy topping on yogurts or cereals.

Buckwheat (GF): Buckwheat isn't related to wheat at all; it's actually a plant similar to rhubarb. When you go to the store to buy buckwheat, you'll have two choices: the pale green groats or the roasted reddish groats often called kasha. Both are hearty and filling, a great source of complex carbohydrates, and wonderful for cold weather eating. If you're new to buckwheat, the milder green groats are an easier sell, as kasha can tend toward a grassier flavor. Buckwheat flour has a beautiful gray to almost purple color and a mild, earthy flavor, making it a star in morning pancakes and crepes.

Bulgur: Bulgur is made by steaming, drying, and then cracking wheat berries—which makes it extremely quick cooking. In fact, it requires little real cooking at all: simply boil water and let the grains steep, covered, off the heat. A common staple in many Middle Eastern recipes, bulgur is a wonderful base for warm grain breakfast bowls—simply add seasonal fruit and a little yogurt and honey, and you're good to go. If you're wondering about the difference between bulgur wheat and cracked wheat, they're close cousins. The only difference is that cracked wheat is made by milling the wheat berry into smaller pieces, whereas bulgur is actually precooked, making it even quicker to cook. When shopping for bulgur, you'll find three different grinds: fine, medium, and coarse. I prefer the coarse grind as it's heartier and chewier, but it does require a slightly longer soaking time.

Couscous: I included couscous in the book although it's not technically a grain—or a pasta. It's essentially tiny little orbs of dough made from the flour of durum wheat. So many folks, including myself, eat it as a grain and it's wonderful in morning recipes, so it made the cut. It's delightfully fluffy and can be purchased in white or whole wheat varieties.

Millet (GF): Resembling little yellow beads, millet has a lovely light texture and is relatively quick cooking because of its small size. I often toast it in a skillet before adding any liquid, as it enhances the nutty flavor of the grain. In terms of texture, some of millet's little beads will cook quicker than others, so you'll likely have some softer grains and some chewy or even crunchy grains (I find this to be a good thing). It's wonderful as a savory porridge with a bit of grated cheese, and it adds immediate crunch when added, uncooked, into cookie dough, granola, muesli, or multigrain cereals. Unlike most grains, I only cook as much millet as I need for a particular recipe (it's a very thirsty grain and leftovers can become quite dry), and I always serve it warm. You will notice millet grits in a few recipes in this book—they're a cracked version of the grain, so they're even quicker cooking, and delightful for a speedy morning porridge.

Oats (GF): There are a few different forms of oats, and each originates from the whole oat berry, or groat. Easy to digest and full of soluble fiber and vitamins B and E, whole-grain oats boast a mild flavor and a pleasant chewy texture and have been a beloved inclusion on the breakfast table for decades—from simple porridges, granola, and muesli to quick breads, muffins, and scones. To learn more about the distinctions between types of oats and when to use them in cooking and baking, see Know Your Oats, page 31. Note: There's a small chance that oats may contain trace amounts of gluten if processed in a facility that also processes wheat. Buy gluten-free oats to be safe if this is a major health concern.

Quinoa (GF): Although usually considered a grain, quinoa is actually a small oval-shaped seed originating from a plant much like spinach. While there are dozens upon dozens of varieties grown in the Andes where quinoa originates, in U.S. stores you'll likely find this quick-cooking grain only in tan, red, or sometimes black varieties (each has a slightly different flavor, so try them all to find your favorite). Regardless of color, quinoa is one of the few plant foods that is a complete protein, so it's become immensely popular with vegetarians and meat eaters alike looking for interesting ways to integrate more protein into their diets. It's a real crowd-pleaser of a grain because it's so quick to cook, gets nice and fluffy, and has an amenable texture. You'll know it's done cooking when the white coiled germ breaks away from the grain, wrapping around each seed. Quinoa makes a great porridge in place of oats, and quinoa flakes can be folded into many baking recipes to add interesting texture and an easy wallop of protein. Always rinse quinoa to slough away any of the bitter coating, saponin (see page 16).

Slow Cooking

Most of the slow-cooking grains cook in 50 to 60 minutes.

Barley: This ancient grain boasts the highest fiber content of all whole grains and has a wonderful nutty flavor. It's sold most commonly as "hulled" or "pearled," but don't let the distinctions throw you. Hulled barley (whole-grain barley) has undergone a process to remove just the outer shell (or hull) leaving the nutritious germ and bran intact. Pearled barley has been processed to remove the germ and most of the bran, giving it a squattier, rounder appearance—like a pearl. Because it's been processed in this way, pearled barley is not technically a whole grain, although I do rely on it in my kitchen and in this book. The reason? It is widely available, cooks more quickly, boasts a wonderful creamy flavor, and remains quite high in fiber. Unlike other grains, barley's fiber isn't housed solely in the bran of the kernel—it's distributed throughout, so there's still ample nutrition in pearled barley. Selecting varieties aside, barley is hard to cook wrong. It soaks up pretty much whatever cooking liquid you give it and has a likable, mild flavor that's as comfortable in morning porridge as it is risotto. Hulled barley is also rolled into quick-cooking flakes (a great substitute for oats in oatmeal), which you'll find in a handful of recipes in this book.

Brown rice (GF): Thousands and thousands of varieties of rice exist worldwide, in a host of different colors and flavors. Conventional white rice has the hull, bran, and germ removed, leaving very little nutritional content. Brown rice, on the other hand, still has the germ and bran so it's much more nutritious. It's what I turn to most often and what you'll find in this book (with recipes calling for long-grain and short-grain brown rice). However, there are many other interesting varieties, such as wild rice or black rice, so feel free to experiment. Just be sure to follow the cooking time and any other special instructions for the variety you're using.

Farro: With twice the fiber of brown rice, a pleasant chewy texture, and a mild earthy flavor, farro is popping up widely on restaurant menus and grocery store shelves. Farro releases some of its starch when cooked, so it becomes almost creamy and doesn't tend to dry out when refrigerated. For this reason, I suggest it as a great starter grain when you're just beginning to experiment with whole grains. Farro is a heartier grain much like wheat berries, so it's nice in warm breakfast bowls or folded into frittatas or omelets. Shopping for farro can be a little confusing as there's debate about whether it's really its own grain or part of a larger wheat family consisting of three ancient varieties: emmer, spelt, and einkorn. Regardless of where you stand on the question, you can make things simpler for yourself by noting that when you shop for farro you'll likely find two options: *perlato* (pearled) and *semi-perlato* (semi-pearled). I usually choose semi-pearled because it has more fiber. Just note that the different varieties have widely varied cooking times, so read the package or bulk bins when you purchase your grains.

Polenta, cornmeal, and grits (GF): There are hundreds of different kinds and shades of corn found in supermarkets around the world, many of which are ground into cornmeal. Polenta and grits are both coarse stone-ground cornmeal, and things can get confusing at the supermarket when shopping for ingredients because the packages you'll find may be labeled either "corn grits" or "polenta." When buying cornmeal, corn grits, or polenta, I make sure that the label reads "whole-grain" (otherwise it's likely not) and avoid "instant" or "quick" varieties, as they don't act the same in most recipes and aren't as nutritious. Stone-ground whole-grain cornmeal comes in a few different grinds (fine, medium, or coarse). For the recipes in this book, I'll always designate which grind would work best. Cornmeal is highly perishable, so try to use it within 6 weeks if storing at room temperature in an airtight container. Store in the refrigerator to draw out the shelf life. For more information on polenta and grits, see page 112.

Steel-cut oats (GF): See page 18.

Wheat berries (wheat family): These raw kernels or "berries" of wheat are where bulgur and cracked wheat originate. Wheat berries are the least processed form of wheat and have a nutty, chewy texture that makes them particularly appealing for heartier dishes like breakfast bowls or scrambles. Look for wheat berries in hard or soft, winter or spring, and red or white; the cooking time will vary a little for each. I usually cook my wheat berries the night before because they can take a chunk of time out of the morning.

COOKING WHOLE GRAINS

In recipes that call for cooked grains, I don't provide cooking instructions within the recipes, which would take up quite a bit of space. Instead, I use a standard general cooking method that's appropriate unless otherwise indicated in the recipe itself or in the Cooking Chart that follows on the next page (the "Good to Know" column will outline variations in cooking method for any one particular grain). The chart offers a very general cooking guide for the grains in this book and the yield you can expect from 1 cup of raw grain. Everyone has preferences on how they like their grains—I tend to like mine on the chewier side, so I use a bit less water than others might instruct. Feel free to adjust as you wish. If your grains are too dry, simply add a little more water, 1 or 2 tablespoons at a time, and cook for an additional few minutes to allow the grains time to absorb the liquid. If your grains have excess liquid at the end of their cooking time, simply drain it away.

Toasting Grains

Before cooking tiny grains like millet and amaranth, I like to toast them because I find they stay pleasantly chewy this way and develop a nice, nutty flavor. To toast, pour the dry grains (don't rinse) into a dry skillet and cook over medium-low heat until they become fragrant (or gently pop, in the case of amaranth), usually 3 to 5 minutes. Because of their small size, they can burn quickly, so be sure to stir occasionally and watch the pan closely. Then proceed to cook as directed.

GENERAL COOKING METHOD

Bring the grains and cooking liquid to a boil, then decrease the heat to a simmer and cover the pot. Don't peek or stir—it will disrupt the steaming of the grains. Simmer until tender, using the cooking times in the chart as a rough guide. If you plan to season with salt, do so toward the end of the cooking time. Allow the grains to sit, covered and away from the heat, for 10 minutes or so, then most grains could benefit from a good fluffing with a fork before using or serving.

QUICK-COOKING GRAINS

GRAIN	WATER	COOK TIME	APPROXIMATE YIELD	GOOD TO KNOW
Amaranth (1 cup / 200 g)	2½ cups	15 to 20 minutes	2 cups	Toast before cooking (optional). Let sit, covered, for 10 minutes off the heat to absorb all liquid.
Buckwheat Groats (1 cup / 180 g)	1½ cups	15 to 20 minutes	3 cups	Buckwheat has a tendency to break apart while cooking. To avoid, toast first with butter or egg before adding water. I prefer butter: Heat 1 tablespoon of butter in a large pot, add the groats, and stir over medium heat for 2 to 3 minutes. Add the cooking liquid and proceed with the general cooking method.
Bulgur, medium/coarse grind (1 cup / 160 g)	1¾ cups	15 minutes	3 cups	Bring the water to a boil, stir in the bulgur, cover, and remove from the heat. Let sit for 10 minutes to absorb the liquid. If you have excess water in the pan after the bulgur is tender, drain it away. Fluff.
Couscous (1 cup / 185 g)	1½ cups	10 minutes	3½ cups	Bring the water to a boil, stir in the couscous, cover, and remove from the heat. Let sit for 10 minutes to absorb the liquid. If you have excess water in the pan after the couscous is tender, drain it away. Fluff.
Millet (1 cup / 180 g)	2 cups	20 to 30 minutes	3 cups	Toast before cooking (optional). Let sit, covered, for 10 minutes off the heat to absorb all liquid.
Oats, rolled (1 cup / 100 g)	1½ cups	10 to 15 minutes	1¾ cups	See specific recipes for notes on preparation. Avoid the temptation to stir while cooking! See Know Your Oats, page 31.
Quinoa (1 cup / 180 g)	1½ cups	15 minutes	3 cups	Rinse before cooking. After cooking, let sit, covered, for 10 minutes off the heat to absorb all liquid, then fluff.

SLOW-COOKING GRAINS

GRAIN	WATER	COOK TIME	APPROXIMATE YIELD	GOOD TO KNOW
Barley, pearled (1 cup / 200 g)	2½ cups	40 to 60 minutes	3 cups	You may soak barley for 2 to 3 hours before cooking for plumper grains. In doing so, you'll likely shave about 15 minutes from the cooking time.
Brown Rice, long-grain (1 cup / 200 g)	1½ cups	35 to 40 minutes	3 cups	This method uses less water and doesn't cook as long, but it yields perfectly chewy rice every time. Allow cooked rice to sit, covered, for 10 minutes off the heat to absorb liquid. Fluff.
Brown Rice, short-grain (1 cup / 210 g)	1¾ cups	40 to 45 minutes	3½ cups	This method uses less water and doesn't cook as long, but it yields perfectly chewy rice every time. Allow cooked rice to sit, covered, for 10 minutes off the heat to absorb liquid. Fluff.
Farro, semi-pearled (1 cup / 185 g)	1¾ cups	25 to 35 minutes	2¾ cups	Cooking time varies widely depending on type of farro, so check the package. If you have excess water in the pan after the farro is tender, drain it away.
Oats, steel-cut (1 cup / 175 g)	3 cups	30 to 35 minutes	3¼ cups	See specific recipes for notes on preparation. Avoid the temptation to stir while cooking! See Know Your Oats, page 31.
Polenta, cornmeal, and stone-ground grits (1 cup / 165 g)	4 cups	20 to 35 minutes	4 cups	Unlike most grains which you should try not to stir while cooking, stir grits and polenta frequently to avoid clumps. Add more water if necessary to avoid clumps or sticking. They are done when the polenta/grits are tender, thick, and creamy.
Wheat Berries (1 cup / 170 g)	2½ cups	50 to 60 minutes	2¾ cups	Cooking time varies widely depending on type of wheat berries, so check the package.

The
BASICS

WHEN I SAT DOWN TO PLAN THIS COOKBOOK, I knew I wanted to write a seasonal breakfast book, but the recipes that initially came to mind were the handful I use in the kitchen most often. The seasonless recipes. The ones that you really want in your morning arsenal whether it's in the heat of August or the quiet gray of February. And so this chapter was born, with many of my favorite breakfast recipes, from homemade yogurt and almond milk to infused honeys and the best oatmeal. While some may require advance prep time, they're meant to be no-fuss, timeless recipes that you will love today— and that you can return to in a few months, or a few years, and love just as much.

Homemade Yogurt

Although it is simple and requires very few ingredients, homemade yogurt takes a little patience at first. Because it is technically a fermented food, yogurt needs a nice warm spot in the house to culture and a good chunk of time (eight to twelve hours—a little less in a yogurt maker, depending on the model). If you're anything like me, you'll fall in love with the planning, the tending, and the fact that you no longer have to buy all of those little expensive containers. I prefer plain whole-milk yogurt, but feel free to use low-fat or nonfat milk if you like. Soy milk, nut milks, or coconut milk will not work for this recipe.

Yogurt is simply milk with added starter (live, good bacteria) that's kept in a warm spot to culture. For your starter, you can use a few tablespoons of store-bought yogurt (just be sure it lists "live and active cultures" in the ingredient list) or dried starter. Many grocery stores stock little packets of dried starter, but you can also order them online (see Sources, page 166). Different store-bought plain yogurts can have very different flavors, so use a yogurt whose taste you like as a starter.

If you eat yogurt a few times a week, a yogurt maker is well worth the investment. With it, making homemade yogurt is as easy as heating milk, tossing in your starter, pouring it into little glass jars, and pressing a button. That being said, you can process yogurt using the "old-fashioned" method without any gadgets or gizmos. I've included both methods for you. MAKES ABOUT 5½ CUPS

A Note on Ingredients: *You'll notice that powdered milk is optional. I use nonfat powdered milk, especially when I'm processing my yogurt the "old-fashioned" way because it really helps the yogurt to firm up. You can absolutely make yogurt without it—it will likely just be on the looser side.*

5 cups / 1.2 L whole milk

¼ cup / 30 g powdered milk, optional (see A Note on Ingredients, above)

3 tablespoons plain yogurt, or 2 to 3 tablespoons powdered starter*

*Read the back of your starter packet for quantity suggestions specific to that particular brand

⇾ Pour the milk into a heavy-bottomed saucepan and, over low heat, bring the temperature up to 185°F. Use a digital-read or candy thermometer to help gauge the temperature. This generally takes about 15 minutes. Don't stir during this time.

⇾ Remove from the heat and vigorously whisk in the powdered milk to get rid of any clumps. Allow the temperature to drop to 115°F. If you want to speed this process up, submerge the saucepan in a sink filled with a few inches of cold water. If your soon-to-be yogurt develops a skin on top, simply skim it off with a spoon and discard.

continued

❧ Once the temperature reaches 115°F, measure out about 1 cup of the warm milk and pour it into a small bowl. Whisk your starter into the small bowl of milk to ensure it gets fully activated. Pour the small bowl of cultured milk back into the large pot of milk and whisk well. Process your yogurt using one of these two methods:

Yogurt Maker Method: Working in batches, pour the milk mixture into a 2-cup liquid measuring cup with a spout and distribute equal amounts between your yogurt maker's small glass jars. Follow the manufacturer's instructions on processing. You can expect a general processing time of 7 to 9 hours. After processing, refrigerate for at least 2 hours before serving.

"Old-Fashioned" Method: To make yogurt using this method, you need a nice warm spot in the house. Many people have luck placing their jars inside a gas oven warmed only by the pilot light. Or maybe you have a really warm laundry room or attic. In my drafty house, I create a cozy little nest with a towel, a mason jar filled with warm water, and a little camping cooler (as small as possible, to maintain a warm temperature).

❧ To begin: Have ready two 1-quart mason jars and lids. Fill one with very hot water and screw on the lid. In the other, pour in the milk mixture and screw on the lid. Wrap the jars snugly in a towel, place in a small cooler, and close the lid. Taking care not to jostle the cooler, set it in the warmest spot in the house. Check progress in 8 hours. On occasion, my yogurt has taken up to 12 hours using this method. The yogurt should be firm but still a touch jiggly. The yogurt will continue to firm up in the refrigerator, so don't worry too much if it appears a little loose. Do note, though, that it will never be as firm as Greek yogurt. Refrigerate for 2 hours before enjoying.

> **Note on Yogurt Thickness:** *If you prefer a Greek-style yogurt, simply strain it. Line a colander with cheesecloth or a very fine-weave dishcloth and place it above a large bowl. Spoon in the yogurt and let sit for 2 to 3 hours in the refrigerator. Discard the liquid (whey) that drains away.*

VANILLA YOGURT: I don't like to add sugar to my yogurt, so this version won't taste like the sweet vanilla yogurt you buy at the market, but it will have just a slight hint of vanilla. Simply add 1 tablespoon pure vanilla extract once the milk reaches 185°F. Proceed as instructed.

MAPLE YOGURT: Add 6 tablespoons Grade B maple syrup to the milk before heating. Proceed as instructed.

FRUIT-ON-THE-BOTTOM YOGURT: Decrease the amount of milk you're using to 4½ cups. In a small nonreactive saucepan, heat 1 cup of your favorite jam over medium-low heat until it comes to a slow, gentle boil. Let it cool to 115°F, then spoon 2 tablespoons of the jam into each jar of your yogurt maker (or spoon all of it into the bottom of your mason jar) right before adding the cooled (to 115°F), cultured milk. Proceed as instructed.

Five-Grain Porridge Mix

My pantry is stocked with jars of different grains, beans, and spices that I keep in the entryway to the kitchen. When the jars of grains get low, I've started to combine the little bits to make porridge. Making your own porridge mix is a wonderful way to become acquainted with different rolled and cracked grains. It's also great to take traveling—if you can track down a stovetop and some boiling water, you've always got a hearty, healthy breakfast. MAKES 3¼ CUPS

Morning Notes: *While I love this particular blend for its different textures and flavors, this is merely a template: if you can't find all five grains, make a three- or four-grain mix instead. Just be sure to use quick-cooking grains (see page 17) like rolled flakes, so you have a relatively uniform porridge (rolled oats, rolled spelt, and quinoa flakes are all great).*

1 cup / 100 g barley flakes

1 cup / 100 g rye flakes

½ cup / 95 g millet grits

½ cup / 60 g cracked wheat

¼ cup / 45 g amaranth

⇥ Combine all the ingredients in a medium bowl and stir to combine. Transfer to an airtight jar for up to 3 months.

⇥ To prepare porridge, see Early Morning Porridge, opposite.

Early Morning Porridge

My sisters and I didn't grow up having morning porridge like many other kids we knew in chilly Northern California. My mom claims it's all she and her sisters ate, so they tired of it quickly and she had little to no desire to make it for us. As an adult though, this has become my go-to rainy- or foggy-day breakfast. This recipe is meant to be something that requires very little thought in the morning—the kind of breakfast that can be prepared when you're only half awake before the day really spins into action. Grab the porridge mix, cook it with water, salt, and cinnamon, and in ten to fifteen minutes— give or take—you're well on your way. SERVES 3 OR 4

Morning Notes: *For a richer porridge, replace half the amount of water with milk. A little pat of butter stirred in at the very end can be nice, too.*

1 cup / 145 g Five-Grain Porridge Mix
   (opposite)
2¾ cups / 660 ml water

¼ teaspoon kosher salt
Generous pinch of ground
   cinnamon (optional)

⇥ Combine all the ingredients in a small saucepan. Bring to a boil over medium heat. Decrease the heat to low, cover, and cook until most of the liquid has been fully absorbed, 12 to 14 minutes. Stir occasionally to prevent clumping. Let sit for 2 to 3 minutes off the heat to fully absorb any additional liquid. Serve warm with your favorite toppings (see page 44).

⇥ While this porridge is at its best right off the stovetop, you can cover and refrigerate it for up to 5 days. To reheat (I do this in the microwave for about 1 minute), be sure to add a spoonful or two of water to rehydrate the grains.

The Very Best Oatmeal

I think the sign of good oatmeal is that you'd consider eating it cold with as much gusto as you would if it were hot. This recipe passes the test. The oats keep their integrity and shape, resulting in what I think of as perfectly cooked, chewy, "blank slate" oats. They resemble a pot of nicely steamed grains more than they do an actual porridge—each bite just begs some doctoring with a little honey and toasted nuts. Many people associate oatmeal with a gummy, gluey texture, so they avoid it. If you're in that camp, I think this recipe just might change your perspective.

I have a few tricks up my sleeve here: First, I find using a bigger pot works best. Even if it seems far too large for the amount of oats, the oats will cook more evenly when less crowded. I toast the oats to bring out their nutty flavor, add the oats only when the water is at a rolling boil, and resist stirring (when you stir your oatmeal, it breaks up the grains and can become gummy). Then I simply turn off the heat and cover the pot—the oats do the rest. It's the perfect recipe for those busy weekday mornings because it's so hands-off. In fact, it will work best the less you fuss with it. SERVES 2 OR 3

Morning Notes: *If you like your oatmeal creamier and in more of a porridge style, simply add more cooking liquid (start with an additional ½ cup and see how you like the texture). Give it a few stirs toward the end of the cooking time, and add even more liquid, 2 tablespoons at a time, until it's right where you like it.*

1 tablespoon unsalted butter

1 cup / 100 g rolled oats

¼ cup / 60 ml milk or nut milk (page 38)

Generous pinch of kosher salt

Pinch of ground cinnamon (optional)

¾ cup plus 1 tablespoon / 195 ml water

Heavy cream, for serving (optional)

Brown sugar, for serving (optional)

⚜ To toast the oats: Melt the butter in a large skillet over medium heat. Add the oats and toast over medium heat, stirring occasionally, until they begin to smell fragrant and nutty, 5 to 7 minutes.

⚜ To cook the oats: In a large heavy-bottomed pot, bring the milk, salt, cinnamon, and water to a slow boil over medium heat. Add the toasted oats and gently stir once or twice to incorporate them into the liquid. Cover the pot and turn off the heat. Allow the oats to sit on the burner for 7 minutes. Don't peek. Don't stir. After 7 minutes, uncover and check the oats. If they're a little wetter than you'd like, allow them to sit in the pot, covered, for another few minutes.

❧ To serve: A simple, classic way to finish this oatmeal is with a splash of cream and a little brown sugar on top. Otherwise, serve with your favorite toppings (see page 44). If some oatmeal is left over, let it cool and store in an airtight container, refrigerated, for up to 5 days. To reheat (I do this in the microwave for about 1 minute), you'll likely need to add a bit more liquid as the oatmeal has a tendency to dry out with time.

Make Ahead: *I often make a double batch of this at the beginning of the week and reheat it in the mornings. Surprisingly, it tastes just as good and ensures I'm not tempted to skip breakfast when things get harried toward the end of the week.*

KNOW YOUR OATS

All varieties of oats begin as whole oat berries (often called groats). They're hulled and then processed in a few different ways—this is where the difference in taste, texture, and cooking times comes into play. In this book, I always designate what kind of oats to use, but elsewhere, if you're unsure, old-fashioned rolled oats are usually a safe bet.

Steel-cut oats: Made by cutting the whole oat groat down into small pieces, steel-cut oats have a charming nubby shape and a wonderful chewy texture. For that reason, I love using them in oatmeal and porridge, but I don't use them in baking recipes because they're quite thick and tend to suck up moisture in ways that can negatively affect your desired outcome. *Cooks in 30 to 40 minutes.*

Rolled oats, or old-fashioned oats: Rolled oats are made by steaming whole oat groats and rolling them out into flakes *before* cutting them to make them more tender. So think of them, really, as oat flakes. They're wonderfully universal: I use them in baking recipes and in my granola and muesli—they cook up beautifully and are easy to find. *Cooks in 10 to 15 minutes.*

Quick-cooking oats: Made much the same way as rolled oats, quick-cooking oats differ only in that they are chopped before they're rolled, so the flakes are even thinner. For this reason, I find them not that satisfying in hot cereals and downright dusty in granola and muesli. I have, in a pinch, used them in cookie recipes but I don't seek them out. *Cooks in 2 minutes.*

Instant oats: In college, I relied on those little brown packages of instant oatmeal. Now I realize that they usually have all kinds of added sugars and flavors and a very generic, uniform texture. Not a good candidate for actual baking recipes.

MARGE GRANOLA

In 2008, I was living just north of San Francisco and was laid off from my job teaching high school English. Instead of allowing myself a few weeks to reflect and think about my next career move, I dove into a job in the catering department at a local restaurant, planning and orchestrating parties and events. Our offices were right above the main kitchen with no natural light or circulating air. To the right of my desk there was a little window that looked down on the bakery, where I'd watch the bakers slice rugelach, roll croissants, hand frost cookies, and crimp pies.

I spent my downtime in the office researching recipes and gawking at the pastries coming out of the oven below. After months of distractedly answering the phone while gazing down at the bustle in the kitchen, I asked Darcy, the head baker, if I could help. And just like that, a new chapter had begun: Sunday mornings were now spent in the bakery. I wasn't used to waking up before dawn. I'd come in clutching my coffee cup and clean apron and spend the first half hour just watching, taking notes, and trying to stay out of the way. I'd splash cream cheese frosting out of the mixer and onto the back wall, drop eggs on the floor, and burn my forearms while taking pans of granola out of the oven. It was chaotic and sweaty and not at all the peaceful, charming place I'd envisioned it would be from my window above. Despite all that, I fell in love with every last bit of it.

After a few months, everything clicked. Recipes became more familiar, the mixer and ovens less foreign, and I learned how to move and communicate in the kitchen. I not only learned how to bake on a commercial scale, but I started to discover what kind of baking I was particularly drawn to: recipes with a tradition and heritage, especially pie. I loved the way pie encouraged you to get acquainted with which fruits were in season and chat with farmers about crops and varietals.

Months passed and I started writing a business plan late at night, fueled by many cups of coffee and an excitement I hadn't felt in a long time. I was going to open a bakery. But wait: I didn't know how to open a bakery. Heck, I didn't even know how to write a business plan. I distracted myself by researching vintage wallpaper and buying antique cake stands. I contacted other bakers to learn about their experiences. I found a broker who drove me around to look at bakery spaces. As anyone who has ever opened a restaurant knows, this is the fun, dreamy part. The rest, the real deal, is much less romantic—so when it came down to the financials behind building out a kitchen and leasing a commercial space, those swatches of vintage wallpaper quickly looked less and less appealing.

In the winter of 2010, I'd figured out a way to begin Marge (named after my maternal grandmother), a version of the business I'd originally envisioned. I rented out a commercial kitchen that I shared with five other small businesses: a tamale maker, a cupcake truck, a falafel truck, a Swedish baker, and a caramel corn producer. I sold pies and other sweets at farmers' markets around the Bay Area every weekend and did local deliveries to businesses and private clients. Business was okay. Pies were expensive and incredibly labor-intensive to make, but I felt like I'd created a little something that was somehow important.

In addition to pies, I started experimenting with an olive oil granola that I'd been eating at home every day. One weekend I had so much extra that I bagged it up, wrapped some baker's twine around each bag, and brought it to the market figuring I could sell a bag or two. I sold twenty bags before 10 a.m. This was big for a sleepy, drizzly Saturday in Marin County. I put the granola up on the Marge website, and within weeks I was researching FedEx rates, printing out shipping labels, and wondering what exactly had just happened. My almost-profitable small pie business morphed into one that actually pays my bills with bags of granola. Before I knew it, I was shipping granola across the country to various retailers and gourmet food shops and supplying it in bulk to local grocery stores.

Marge Granola has feet of her own now. One graduate degree, one adjunct professorship, and two high school teaching jobs later, I'm suddenly a baker and business owner. It's not what I planned or envisioned for myself, but I've stumbled upon a delicious product that people truly love, and I'm delighted that I get to be a part of so many mornings. Most of all, I'm excited to share a few of the recipes with you in this book.

Make-Your-Own Signature Granola

When you start making granola at home, something happens: you begin to develop your own tweaks and preferences, and before you know it you have a signature blend. While we have a set line of flavors and recipes in the Marge kitchen today, here is my formula to tinker with at home using your favorite ingredients. You need oats, sweetener, spices, and a bit of oil to make granola, so that's your blueprint. Then modify as you like based on what tastes good to you. This recipe is special because it's made with olive oil, has a little more salt than most granola recipes, and is loaded with good nuts and seeds. It's nice and toasty, straddling the line between sweet and savory—perfect in the morning or by the handful in the afternoon. For some inspiration on nuts, seeds, and fruit that are great in granola, see Toppings and Stir-Ins, page 44; for tips on making granola, see page 144.

MAKES 8 TO 9 CUPS

3 cups / 300 g rolled oats

2½ cups raw nuts or seeds, or a mixture

1½ teaspoons kosher salt

¼ teaspoon ground cinnamon

½ teaspoon ground cardamom

½ cup / 120 ml oil (I use extra-virgin olive oil)

½ cup plus 1 tablespoon / 135 ml liquid sweetener (such as honey or maple syrup)

¾ teaspoon pure vanilla extract

¾ cup chopped dried fruit

⇥ Preheat the oven to 350°F. Line a 13 by 18-inch baking sheet with parchment paper or a silicone mat.

⇥ Mix the oats, nuts and seeds, salt, cinnamon, and cardamom together in a large bowl. Stir to combine. Add the oil, sweetener, and vanilla and stir again to combine fully.

⇥ Turn the granola out onto the prepared pan and spread in an even layer. Bake until the mixture is light brown and fragrant, 35 to 40 minutes, stirring every 15 or 20 minutes to make sure the granola cooks evenly. (It might not seem as toasty as you'd like it when done, but it firms up as it cools.)

⇥ Remove from the oven and let cool completely on the pan. Stir in the dried fruit. Store in an airtight container at room temperature for 3 to 4 weeks or in the refrigerator for up to 6 weeks. The granola also freezes beautifully for up to 3 months.

Whole-Grain Pancake Mix

I grew up on Bisquick. It reminds me of Sunday mornings at the kitchen counter with my dad. While the ingredients leave much to be desired (relying on hydrogenated oils), I harbor no hard feelings toward the big yellow box, and nothing beats the ease of having a mix all ready to go. But these days instead of Bisquick, I whisk together this whole-grain mix once every month or so and keep it in a big glass jar in the pantry. Folding rolled oats into pancakes gives them a hearty, toothsome quality that I love. Some folks prefer a more uniform, smooth pancake and grind the oats down in a food processor before adding them. Choose your route, but I urge you to try the version below first. I have a feeling you might like them. MAKES ABOUT 4 CUPS; 4 BATCHES WHOLE-GRAIN BUTTERMILK PANCAKES (PAGE 36)

2 cups / 240 g unbleached
   all-purpose flour

¾ cup / 100 g buckwheat flour

½ cup / 60 g spelt flour

¾ cup / 75 g rolled oats

3 tablespoons natural cane sugar

2 tablespoons baking powder

2 teaspoons baking soda

½ teaspoon kosher salt

In a large bowl, stir together all the ingredients. Scoop into a large resealable plastic bag or a large glass jar and store for 6 to 8 weeks. Refrigerate for longer shelf life (3 to 4 months). Give the mix a good stir before using it to integrate any ingredients that may have settled.

Whole-Grain Buttermilk Pancakes

So many pancakes made with all white flour are fluffy but taste largely like whatever you top them with, while so many whole-grain pancakes end up tasting great but cook up flat and dense. This recipe offers the best of both: it yields relatively fluffy pancakes boasting a nice, earthy flavor from the whole-grain flours. While I've been known to add grated fruit like apples or pears to the batter, I tend to serve these pancakes as they are, simply topped with a little butter, honey, and seasonal fruit. MAKES 9 OR 10 PANCAKES

Morning Notes: *I like to cook these pancakes to order, but I also like to sit down and eat together with friends. Luckily, you can warm them in a 200°F oven for up to 30 minutes without drying them out.*

1 large egg

½ cup / 120 ml milk

½ cup / 120 ml buttermilk

1 tablespoon butter, melted and slightly cooled, plus more for greasing the pan and for serving

1 cup / 165 g Whole-Grain Pancake Mix (page 35)

Honey or maple syrup, for serving

⇥ In a small bowl, whisk together the egg, milk, buttermilk, and butter. Whisk the pancake mix into the milk mixture until smooth. Let the batter rest for 10 minutes to allow the dry ingredients to soak up some of the liquid. If the batter feels far too thick and difficult to easily whisk or stir, add 1 tablespoon more milk or water to loosen it up.

⇥ Melt a nub of butter in a large skillet or griddle over medium heat (you want the melted butter to completely coat the pan). Scoop ¼ cup of batter into the pan. Repeat, depending on the size of your pan. Cook each pancake until the bottom is golden brown and the top begins to bubble, 2 to 3 minutes. Flip and cook the other side an additional 1 to 2 minutes. You'll likely need another bit of butter in the pan in between batches. Serve warm, topped with butter, honey, or maple syrup, as desired.

Make Ahead: *You can make the batter and store it, covered, in the refrigerator for up to 1 day. You'll probably need to add 1 to 2 tablespoons more milk or water to loosen it up after it sits overnight.*

Two Easy Nut Milks: Almond *and* Hazelnut

When people move to Boulder, Colorado, nut milk is most likely in their future. Or that's how it seemed to me during my college years in that charming town, where I drank my fair share stirred into coffee and tea. To this day, I still love the rich taste of almond and hazelnut milk, but I've developed a Boulder-like aversion to the additives found in many store-bought brands. Today I make my own—a simple process, but also one that requires a little downtime for the nuts to soak. So plan ahead. It's normal for homemade nut milk to separate in the refrigerator, so give it a good shake before using. Try these milks in Warm Farro Breakfast Bowl with Apples, Cranberries, and Hazelnuts (page 109) or with Dried Cherry, Almond, and Flax Muesli (page 82). MAKES ABOUT 3 CUPS

1 cup / 140 g raw almonds, or
1 cup / 120 g raw hazelnuts

3 cups / 720 ml water
1 to 2 tablespoons honey (optional)

❧ To prepare the nuts: Soak the nuts at room temperature in enough water to fully cover them for at least 6 hours and up to overnight. After soaking, drain them in a colander and rinse well with fresh water. Put the nuts, 3 cups water, and the honey in a blender. Blend on high speed until the nuts are pulverized and the mixture is smooth, about 1 minute. Let sit for 10 minutes.

❧ To strain the milk: Drape a piece of fine-weave cheesecloth inside a colander (or use a nut milk bag) and place a large pot below to catch the strained nut milk. Pour the milk into the lined colander. You can apply some pressure with a wooden spoon to encourage every last bit of milk to strain through. Pour the liquid into a glass jar or other airtight container and store in the refrigerator for up to 3 days.

VANILLA ALMOND MILK: Before blending the almonds, split one vanilla bean and scrape the seeds into the blender (or use 1 teaspoon pure vanilla extract) and proceed as instructed. Discard the pod.

CHOCOLATE HAZELNUT MILK: Add 2 tablespoons honey and 2 tablespoons unsweetened cocoa powder along with a pinch of salt to the blender with the hazelnuts and water, and proceed as instructed. Note that your hazelnut pulp will be laced with cocoa, so keep that in mind if you plan to dry it and use it in a baking recipe (see opposite).

WHAT TO DO WITH THAT LEFTOVER NUT PULP?

You'll be left with a lot of almond or hazelnut pulp when you drain nut milk. I can never bear to discard it. In the warmer summer months, I use it as compost in the garden, but in the cooler months when I don't mind having my oven on for a long time, I'll dry it out to make almond meal or hazelnut meal, which is wonderful in cookies, quick breads, and muffins.

To dry out the pulp, set your oven on the lowest setting possible (for me, it's 170°F). Spread the pulp in an even layer on a baking sheet lined with parchment paper or a silicone mat. Put it in the oven and leave the oven door cracked an inch or so. Dry out the pulp until it's crumbly, 6 to 7 hours. For a finer texture, pulse the dried meal in a food processor a few times.

Infused Honeys

Throughout the year, infused honeys are a great way to customize what you swirl into your hot and cold cereals and yogurts. Many people let their honey slowly steep with herbs or spices for a week or two on a windowsill, but I've found a quicker method: heating the honey with the infusions. It works just as well and is immediately gratifying. Look for a light, mild-flavored honey like clover or alfalfa.

Here are a few seasonal suggestions, but feel free to use whatever herbs and spices sound most appealing to you. Lavender, rose petals, lemon balm, basil, ginger, sage, cinnamon, rosemary, and thyme would all be wonderful. Regardless of the ingredients you choose, you want to slowly heat the honey and infusions together and not let them boil. As the honey warms, it will thin a little and become quite fragrant, and when it cools, it will firm up like the honey you know and love (but better). MAKES ABOUT 1 CUP

> **Morning Notes:** *There are different theories on how long infused honey can be kept safely. Honey on its own has an infinite shelf life, but when you introduce other substances like herbs and flowers, there's a small chance the honey could spoil. This is more likely with fresh herbs because the moisture can cause the growth of undesirable spores. Because I'm overly cautious when it comes to these things, I try to use the infused honeys within 3 to 4 weeks.*

Spring: Chamomile Honey

For this infusion, I fill a small cloth tea bag with chamomile flowers so the honey stays clean of particles. You should be able to find both the cloth bags and the chamomile at herb and tea shops or well-stocked grocery stores, and also online (see Sources, page 166).

¼ cup / 5 g dried chamomile flowers
1 cup / 240 ml honey

꙳ Place the chamomile flowers in a cloth tea bag or small bundle of cheesecloth. Make sure the flowers are pushed toward the bottom of the bag so they'll be truly immersed in the honey. In a small saucepan over medium-low heat, warm the honey and flowers together for 5 minutes. Don't let the honey come to a full boil. If it starts to boil, decrease the heat to low. Remove from the heat and let the mixture sit in the pan for 20 minutes to really give the flavors a chance to infuse. Remove the tea bag, making sure to squeeze all of the flavorful honey from it before discarding. Pour the honey into a glass jar for storage.

Summer: Vanilla Bean Honey

This fragrant speckled honey is my go-to for everything from pancakes to Earl Grey tea.

1 cup / 240 ml honey
1 vanilla bean, split

❧ Pour the honey into a small saucepan and place on the stove. Scrape the seeds from the vanilla bean into the honey and add the pod to it as well for extra flavor. Over medium-low heat, warm the honey and vanilla together for 5 minutes. Don't let the honey come to a full boil. If it starts to boil, decrease the heat to low. Remove from the heat and let the mixture sit in the pan for 20 minutes to really give the flavors a chance to infuse. Remove and discard the vanilla bean pod and pour the honey into a glass jar for storage.

continued

Fall: Chai-Spiced Honey

I look forward to the first cool, crisp mornings in October, when I drizzle this warmly spiced honey on porridge and oatmeal.

1 cup / 240 ml honey
4 star anise pods
3 cinnamon sticks
3 cardamom pods
10 peppercorns
4 cloves

❧ In a small saucepan over medium-low heat, warm all the ingredients together for 5 minutes. Don't let the honey come to a full boil. If it starts to boil, decrease the heat to low. Remove from the heat and let the mixture sit in the pan for 20 minutes to really give the flavors a chance to infuse. Using a fine-mesh sieve, strain the honey and pour it into a glass jar for storage.

Winter: Triple-Citrus Honey

You can use the zest of any citrus you'd like here. I've made this honey with just lemon zest, and it's wonderful and bright, but I love this combination of three fruits.

1 cup / 240 ml honey
1 tablespoon grated lemon zest
1 tablespoon grated tangerine zest
1 tablespoon grated grapefruit zest

❧ In a small saucepan over medium-low heat, warm all the ingredients together for 5 minutes. Don't let the honey come to a full boil. If it starts to come to a boil, decrease the heat to low. Remove from the heat and let sit in the pan for 20 minutes to really give the flavors a chance to infuse. Using a fine-mesh sieve, strain the honey and pour it into a glass jar for storage.

Quinoa Crunch

Think of this recipe as a riff on a quick granola, but made with quinoa instead of oats. Strewn with almonds and sesame seeds, this crunchy mix turns a simple bowl of yogurt into something almost regal. Plus, the quick punch of protein will help tide you over until lunch. In addition to draining the rinsed quinoa, I also spread it out on a clean, dry kitchen towel to fully dry. No one wants to be working with soggy quinoa.

MAKES 1½ CUPS

1 cup / 180 g quinoa, rinsed and drained well (see page 16)

½ cup / 40 g sliced raw almonds

3 tablespoons raw sesame seeds

1 tablespoon maple syrup

1 tablespoon safflower or canola oil

⁂ Preheat the oven to 375°F. Line a baking sheet with parchment paper or a silicone mat.

⁂ Mix all the ingredients and spread on the prepared baking sheet. Bake until toasty and fragrant, 10 to 12 minutes.

⁂ Transfer to a bowl and let cool completely. Store in an airtight container at room temperature for up to 1 month.

TOPPINGS AND STIR-INS

For most of the recipes in this book, I've provided topping suggestions, but it's nice to have a big list for when you draw a blank or find yourself in a morning rut. These additions work for oatmeal, porridge, pancakes, waffles, and warm whole-grain bowls. After a little experimenting, you'll start to view the grains as a jumping-off point and the toppings and stir-ins as a way to really dress them up.

Fresh

- Pomegranate seeds
- Orange or tangerine wedges
- Seasonal berries
- Sliced banana, figs, or dates
- Grated apple or pear

Crunchy

- Quinoa Crunch (page 43)
- Cacao nibs
- Popped amaranth (see page 128)
- Toasted millet (see page 79)
- Granola (pages 34, 57, and 145)
- Chopped peanuts
- Sesame seeds, poppy seeds, or ground flaxseeds
- Toasted nuts, such as walnuts, hazelnuts, pecans, or almonds
- Raw cashews, pepitas, or pistachios
- Toasted coconut flakes

Smooth

- Yogurt
- Nut milks, like almond or hazelnut milk (page 38)
- Milk, buttermilk, or soy milk
- Coconut milk
- Crème fraîche
- Mascarpone cheese
- Lemony Yogurt Sauce (page 72)

The Sweet Side

- Brown sugar
- Maple syrup
- Infused honeys (page 40)
- Molasses
- Apple butter
- Apricot Cherry Compote (page 98)
- Blueberry Sauce (page 101)
- Roasted Black Cherries (page 99)
- Stewed Red Currants (page 100)
- Honeyed Ricotta (page 131)
- Strawberry Rhubarb Quick Jam (page 71)
- Chunky Maple Almond Butter (page 163)
- Dark Chocolate Hazelnut Spread (page 133)
- Spiced Pear Sauce (page 134)
- Orange zest
- Crystallized ginger
- Melted coconut oil
- Dried cranberries, cherries, or apricots
- Raisins, currants, or chopped dates
- Chopped dried mango or papaya

The Savory Side

- Good butter
- Balsamic vinegar
- Fresh herbs, such as parsley, chives, or dill
- Chopped green onions
- Grated Parmesan cheese, sea salt, or black pepper
- Rehydrated sun-dried tomatoes
- Sautéed mushrooms and leeks
- Eggs (fried or poached, see page 86)
- Flaky salt

A Few of My Favorite Seasonal Combinations

These toppings are a little more deluxe, but they're tried-and-true favorites—great with morning oats, porridge, or warm grain bowls. Once you start experimenting, you'll find in no time that you have your favorites, too.

Spring

- Fresh mango, coconut milk, toasted coconut flakes, and crushed pistachios
- Fresh strawberries, Honeyed Ricotta (page 131), and graham cracker crumbs
- Stewed Red Currants (page 100), Greek yogurt, and honey

Summer

- Chopped green onions, sesame seeds, extra-virgin olive oil, sea salt, and black pepper
- Roasted Black Cherries (page 99), mascarpone cheese, toasted hazelnuts, and cacao nibs
- Fresh peaches, blueberries, vanilla extract, lemon zest, and cream

Fall

- Pumpkin puree, muscovado sugar, toasted pecans, pumpkin pie spice, and whole milk
- Figs, honey, toasted almonds, and popped amaranth (see page 128)
- Spiced Pear Sauce (page 134), ground cardamom, and Honeyed Ricotta (page 131)

Winter

- Golden raisins, coconut milk, ground cardamom, and crystallized ginger
- Sliced banana, peanut butter, and honey
- Crumbled bacon, grated Gruyère cheese, chopped fresh parsley, warm milk, and sea salt

SPRING
coasting

BUSY WEEKDAYS

Dried Mango and Toasted Coconut Muesli 50

Cherry Hazelnut Quinoa Bars 52

Cheesy Chive Millet Grits 54

Rocky Mountain Couscous 55

BRUNCH

Smoked Salmon Crème Fraîche Tart
with a Cornmeal Millet Crust 63

Bacon and Kale Polenta Squares 65

Strawberry Oat Breakfast Crisp 66

Triple-Coconut Quinoa Porridge 68

SLOW SUNDAYS

Apricot Pistachio Granola 57

Oven-Baked Asparagus, Pea, and Farro Frittata 58

California Barley Bowl
with Lemony Yogurt Sauce 60

SPREADS AND TOPPINGS

Strawberry Rhubarb Quick Jam 71

Lemony Yogurt Sauce 72

Green Herb Sauce 73

WHEN I WAS GROWING UP, John and Maggie, my parent's hippie friends from Oregon, would stay for weeks at a time in our old, creaky Victorian house. My family's routine of school, naps, and meals flew right out the door whenever they arrived, replaced instead with whimsy and spontaneity. With Maggie I'd watch *The Brady Bunch* and eat frozen cookie dough on the couch; with John I learned to ride my first bike. He'd tuck daisies behind my ears each time we'd stop to rest, one day finally taking his hands off the back of the seat to let me coast down the sidewalk, moving forward on my own.

I've had that same feeling for the past few decades, minus the daisies and the pink banana seat. As is the case with many people in their twenties, I moved around a lot. I attended a few different colleges and lived in too many apartments to count on both hands. There were numerous U-Hauls, pricey security deposits, messy roommates, messy roommates' boyfriends, clanky heaters, and noisy neighbors. In each new place, I'd find myself turning first to the kitchen in order to make myself feel at home. If the plates were neatly stacked, the teapot set on the stove, and the glasses all just so, things would be okay.

Until they weren't. In my early thirties, a long relationship ended suddenly with me sitting inside a big San Francisco apartment alone, wondering what to do next. After days of barely sleeping or eating, I packed up yet another moving truck—this time with my eyes set on my mom's house just across the Golden Gate Bridge in Marin County. At first I felt like I'd failed somehow, like moving back home meant I was throwing in the towel. But I kept busy. Very busy.

I started my small baking business, Marge, in my mother's kitchen that year. My mom was my best taste tester and a most patient witness to the whirlwind of sugar and butter that had suddenly taken over her kitchen. I moved out of her house and into a charming apartment across the bay in Oakland a year later as February's cherry blossoms bloomed fiercely, the mornings getting warm enough for iced coffee and bare feet. After paying the movers, I looked around at all the boxes in the living room and chose instead to begin with the kitchen. Later that day, I picked up pink peonies at the corner market, made tea, and sat down to rest for what felt like the first time in days.

The view from the kitchen table wasn't grand. It overlooked a rusty fire escape and the towering brick building next door. Instead of a nicely groomed lawn like most of the residences on our street, the neighbors had nothing more than barbed wire and a tangled patch of daisies. And while the task of unpacking boxes still loomed, sitting in my peaceful kitchen staring out at the little white and yellow flowers made me think of John and that first feeling of moving forward, knowing that once again, everything would be just fine.

SEASONAL *Spotlight*

Tender, plump **apricots** are a spring fruit that easily make their way into the kitchen. In California, it was easy to find the sweet, special Blenheim or Royal apricots as fresh fruit; in Seattle, I encounter them more in jams. Apricots bruise very easily, so store them in a paper bag on the counter and try to eat (or use) them quickly. I look forward to the season's first **rhubarb** for months. The tart pink stalks are wonderful roasted or baked and spooned atop yogurt, toast, and scones. I buy a bunch at the market and chop and freeze bags of it so I can fold the chunks into pies, muffins, and cakes throughout the year. **Strawberries** are easy to come by year-round, but buy them locally at the farmers' market in the spring and summer. They're sweeter, often smaller, and perfect sliced as is.

A member of the onion family, **leeks** add a subtle sweet flavor to spring recipes like quiche, slow-scrambled eggs, simple soups, and delicate pastas. Most people use the white and light green parts only, as they're most flavorful; be sure to wash your leeks well between the layers to remove sand and grit. Sweet and tender fresh **peas** are always a sign that spring has truly arrived. And vibrant, tender **asparagus** in shades of green, purple, or white is another sign that spring is here. When choosing a good bunch, look for firm stalks and avoid flowering tips.

Dried Mango *and* Toasted Coconut Muesli

Rather than simply being a mixture of raw oats, nuts, and seeds, this muesli is toasted with just a touch of honey and oil, resulting in a crunchy base for your favorite yogurt, kefir, or milk. In February and March, when spring fruits haven't crept into the markets and the days are gray and wet, I use a lot of vibrant dried fruits to trick my senses—here the combination of pepitas (aka pumpkin seeds) and beautiful orange mango makes for a pretty and decidedly healthy way to begin each morning. MAKES ABOUT 4 CUPS

Morning Notes: *If you're not familiar with rye flakes, they look (and act) just like rolled oats, but they're a bit darker in color and have a lovely, earthy flavor. You'll likely find them right next to the oats in the bulk bins at any well-stocked grocery store.*

1¼ cups / 125 g rye flakes

1 cup / 100 g rolled oats

½ cup / 65 g raw pepitas

¼ cup / 15 g wheat bran

¼ teaspoon kosher salt

½ cup / 25 g unsweetened
  coconut flakes

¼ teaspoon ground cinnamon
  (optional)

¼ cup / 60 ml honey, plus more
  for serving

2 tablespoons coconut oil
  or extra-virgin olive oil

½ cup / 60 g chopped dried mango

Milk or yogurt, for serving

Honey, for serving

Preheat the oven to 325°F. Line a rimmed baking sheet with parchment paper or a silicone mat.

In a medium bowl, stir together the rye flakes, rolled oats, pepitas, wheat bran, salt, coconut flakes, and cinnamon.

Heat the honey and coconut oil in a small saucepan over low heat until warmed. Pour the mixture into the dry ingredients and stir until combined (you can use your hands to help here). Spread evenly across the prepared baking sheet and bake until golden brown, 20 to 25 minutes, stirring occasionally to ensure it's cooked evenly. Remove from the oven and let cool completely on the baking sheet. Add the dried mango and stir to combine.

Serve with milk or yogurt and a generous drizzle of honey. While many people soak their muesli, I wouldn't with this one, as the pleasant toasty-ness will really get lost. If stored in an airtight container at room temperature, muesli will remain fresh for at least 3 weeks.

Cherry Hazelnut Quinoa Bars

These simple no-bake energy bars are great for on-the-go mornings, but they sneak easily into afternoon and evening territory given the hint of cocoa. Sweetened solely with soft dates and dried cherries, these bars also pack a little hit of protein from the quinoa flakes and nuts. While this recipe couldn't be much easier, you do need to let these bars set up in the refrigerator for 2 hours before slicing. MAKES 12 BARS

Morning Notes: *Quinoa flakes are essentially quinoa that has been steamed and rolled into quick-cooking flakes. I like to fold them into baked goods and pancakes or use them as another morning porridge option. Feel free to substitute rolled oats instead.*

½ cup / 60 g sesame seeds, toasted (see page 12) and cooled

2 cups / 240 g hazelnuts, toasted and skinned (see page 12) and cooled

20 Medjool dates, pitted and chopped (about 2 cups / 325 g)

1 cup / 140 g dried cherries

Generous pinch of kosher salt

½ teaspoon pure vanilla extract

½ teaspoon ground cinnamon

1 tablespoon unsweetened cocoa powder

½ cup / 40 g quinoa flakes

⇥ Line an 8-inch square baking pan with enough parchment paper so that it hangs over each side.

⇥ Put the sesame seeds, hazelnuts, dates, dried cherries, salt, vanilla, cinnamon, and cocoa powder in the bowl of a food processor fitted with the metal blade (it will be quite full, but the mixture blends down quickly). If you have a smaller food processor, you can blend the ingredients in several batches. Process continuously until the mixture has come together in one ball, 2 to 3 minutes. Stop the machine and scrape down the sides every now and then as needed.

⇥ Turn the mixture out into a medium bowl and add the quinoa flakes. I use my hands to knead the mixture so the flakes are thoroughly incorporated. Transfer to the prepared pan and spread in an even layer. Use your hands or the back of a spatula to press down and create an even, firm layer. Refrigerate for at least 2 hours (or freeze for 1 hour, if in a hurry).

⇥ When ready to slice, lift the bars out of the pan by grabbing the overhanging parchment paper. Cut into small bars (about 2 by 3 inches). Refrigerate in an airtight container for up to 7 days. Alternatively, wrap individually in plastic wrap and freeze for up to 3 months.

Make It Your Own: *Don't like hazelnuts? Use almonds instead. Not a fan of dried cherries? Feel free to use dried apricots or an additional 1 cup of dates. For more of a treat, fold in bits of dark chocolate along with the quinoa flakes.*

A TALE OF TWO CITIES: *San Francisco and Seattle*

As I walked home on a cool spring evening in Oakland, Sam called, the Seattle web design-er that I'd hired to help my baking business, Marge. This was odd only because he'd already finished the website and I knew I'd sent in my final payment. That night, Sam asked how I was settling into my new apartment. He listened while I nervously droned on and on about new furniture and freeway access and the twenty-four-hour donut shop right down the hill. There was silence on the other line. "How's your heart, Megan?" he asked.

It was a question that deserved a genuine answer. And so it began. A spring filled with late-night texting, eventual Skyping, simultaneous book reading, postcards and packages, letters and longing. In April, Sam visited the Bay Area for the first time.

The two weeks that followed were filled with grand tourist gestures and the delicious meals and moments that make up daily life. And then Sam went home. We both sat in our respective apartments feeling an undeniable emptiness, and we promptly scheduled another visit. My time in Seattle and his subsequent visits to the Bay Area became routine for us—and after many months, we started to talk about who would move where.

But in the midst of all the back-and-forth trips, there were always mornings. Sunny or blustery with rain, in California or in Washington, we'd lounge on the couch with the paper and coffee or visit the farmers' market. In San Francisco there were morning buns and fluffy slices of quiche at Tartine, sunny naps in Dolores Park, and record shopping. In Seattle there were flaky croissants at Café Besalu, Sam's pancakes and pots of tea, and walks around Green Lake.

Regardless of geography, waking up to another morning in each others' company felt like home. And so, early the following year, yet another U-Haul was packed to head north.

Cheesy Chive Millet Grits

Millet grits are simply whole millet grains that have been ground, making them very quick cooking and perfect for a speedy savory porridge. I buy mine from Bob's Red Mill (see Sources, page 166). You can fold in just about any cheese you'd like here. I've tried this with a creamy goat cheese, a salty Parmesan, and a nutty Gruyère. You just want to make sure you're using a cheese that melts well, so avoid firm cheeses like paneer or halloumi. My go-to is a nice sharp Cheddar. It seems most traditional, and while I'm often tasked with coming up with recipe ideas that use interesting and innovative flavor combinations, sometimes tradition is comforting—as is the case with this recipe. SERVES 4

2 cups / 480 ml water

1 cup / 240 ml milk

2 tablespoons extra-virgin olive oil, plus more for serving

¾ teaspoon kosher salt

1 cup / 190 g millet grits

Freshly ground black pepper

1¼ cups / 90 g grated sharp Cheddar cheese

2 tablespoons chopped fresh chives

⌇ In a saucepan over medium heat, combine the water, milk, olive oil, and salt and bring to a gentle boil. Add the millet grits, stir well, and decrease the temperature to low. Cover and cook until thick and creamy, 10 to 15 minutes, stirring occasionally to avoid sticking or clumping. If the grits seem too thick and you're unable to stir them easily, add more water, 2 tablespoons at a time, until the consistency is as you'd like. Taste and season with additional salt, if you'd like, and pepper.

⌇ Remove from the heat and stir in the Cheddar cheese until melted and creamy. Just before serving, fold in the chives. Serve hot.

Make It Your Own: *To dress this up in the winter, I like to rehydrate sun-dried tomatoes in warm water (you can use oil-packed if you prefer); they add a pop of color and an earthy sweetness. Or in the summer, infuse a bunch of basil in a small jar of olive oil for a few days and drizzle the herby oil over these grits.*

Rocky Mountain Couscous

I remember going out to breakfast with my dad as a little girl and seeing Denver omelets on the menu everywhere—from our small-town diner, Betty Mae's, to a hotel lobby on any given road trip. When I moved to Colorado for college, I started to see them once again. I'm here to tell you: the Denver omelet is alive and well in Colorado. This savory morning couscous is in memory of those very years—years that featured onions, peppers, and ham in everything from muffins and quick breads to pastas and pizzas. SERVES 4

Morning Notes: *Avoid using thin slices of sandwich meat here; you want larger, chunkier pieces of ham that won't get lost in the mix. I always have my local butcher slice a very thick wedge of deli ham for me. Then I finely dice it at home.*

2 tablespoons extra-virgin olive oil

¾ cup / 90 g diced yellow onion
(about 1 small onion)

¾ cup / 90 g diced green bell pepper
(about ½ large pepper)

4 ounces / 115 g cooked ham steak,
diced into small cubes
(scant 1 cup / 240 ml)

2¾ cups / 400 g cooked whole wheat
couscous (see page 22)

¾ teaspoon kosher salt

Freshly ground black pepper

¼ cup / 5 g finely chopped fresh
flat-leaf parsley (optional)

¾ cup / 55 g grated sharp
Cheddar cheese

3 green onions, finely chopped (about
3 tablespoons), for serving (optional)

Hot sauce, for serving (optional)

⌇ In a saucepan over medium heat, warm the olive oil until shimmering. Sauté the onion and bell pepper until soft, about 5 minutes. Stir in the ham and cook over medium heat until warmed through. Fold in the cooked couscous and decrease the heat to low. Add the salt and a few grinds of pepper and stir well. Taste and season further if you'd like. Remove from the heat.

⌇ Stir in the parsley. Sprinkle the Cheddar cheese on top of the couscous and cover the pan. The cheese will begin to melt after just a few minutes. Stir to incorporate the cheese as much as possible. Scoop a large serving of couscous into each bowl and top with the green onions and a bit of hot sauce. If covered and refrigerated, the couscous will keep for 3 to 4 days.

Apricot Pistachio Granola

This is a version of the granola that the *Wall Street Journal* wrote about on a Saturday morning in early June of 2012. Once you develop product flavors for a business, you don't get to continue altering them once the packaging is printed and customers fall in love with it. However, I've taken to adding sunflower seeds and crystallized ginger when I make this at home. For my tips and tricks on making the best granola, see page 144.

MAKES ABOUT 8 CUPS

Morning Notes: *Buying apricots from bulk bins with a high turnover is always a good bet because they're likely much fresher than packaged dried fruits. You can also buy diced dried apricots, which is what I do for Marge (see Sources, page 166).*

3 cups / 300 g rolled oats

1 cup / 130 g raw pistachios, coarsely chopped

1 cup / 130 g raw pepitas

$^1\!/_2$ cup / 60 g raw sesame seeds

$^1\!/_2$ cup / 60 g raw sunflower seeds

1 teaspoon kosher salt

$^1\!/_4$ teaspoon ground cinnamon

$^1\!/_2$ teaspoon ground cardamom

$^1\!/_2$ teaspoon pure vanilla extract

$^1\!/_2$ cup / 120 ml extra-virgin olive oil

$^1\!/_2$ cup / 120 ml maple syrup

$^1\!/_2$ cup / 75 g finely chopped dried apricots (about 10 dried apricots)

$^1\!/_4$ cup / 25 g diced crystallized ginger

⇥ Preheat the oven to 325°F. Line a large rimmed baking sheet with parchment paper or a silicone mat.

⇥ In a large bowl, stir together the oats, pistachios, pepitas, sesame seeds, sunflower seeds, salt, cinnamon, and cardamom.

⇥ Add the vanilla, olive oil, and maple syrup and stir to combine. I use my hands at this point so that all of the wet and dry ingredients are evenly mixed together. Turn the mixture out onto the prepared baking sheet and spread in an even layer.

⇥ Bake until fragrant and golden brown, 35 to 40 minutes. Stir every 15 to 20 minutes to ensure the granola bakes evenly. Remove from the oven and let cool completely on the baking sheet. If the granola doesn't seem as toasty and crunchy as you'd like, it will firm up considerably as it cools. Stir in the apricots and crystallized ginger once the granola has cooled. Store in an airtight container for 3 to 4 weeks or refrigerate for up to 6 weeks (if refrigerating, keep the apricots in a separate sealed bag and add them as you enjoy your granola so they don't become hard and dry.

Make It Your Own: *Love this granola but ready to branch out? For a template for making your own signature granola flavor, see page 34.*

Oven-Baked Asparagus, Pea, and Farro Frittata

I first realized the seasons were different in Seattle when Sam and I visited the farmers' market in the early spring about a month after I'd moved north. We strolled down the narrow street and grabbed a cup of coffee, then I turned to him and asked where they keep all of the citrus. He looked at me sweetly and told me that they don't grow citrus in Washington. Instead, early spring in Seattle means lots of greens and root vegetables, with seasonal staples like stone fruits and fava beans peering out much later than I was accustomed to in the Bay Area. Consequently, this is very much a late spring frittata for us now, and a most welcome hit of color on those frequent gray mornings. SERVES 6

Morning Notes: For this recipe, you're baking the frittata in the same pan used to sauté the asparagus and peas, so seek out a medium ovenproof skillet. I use my 10-inch cast-iron pan and it bakes up a beautiful frittata with nicely browned edges. Also, if you're using thawed frozen peas, you'll add them after cooking the asparagus, whereas if you're using fresh peas, you'll cook them along with the asparagus.

2 tablespoons extra-virgin olive oil

¼ cup / 25 g minced shallot
(about 1 large shallot)

1 pound / 450 g asparagus, tough ends removed, sliced on the diagonal (about 2 cups sliced / 230 g)

½ cup / 60 g fresh peas
or thawed frozen peas

6 large eggs, beaten

¼ cup / 60 ml whole milk

¼ cup / 15 g grated Parmesan cheese

½ teaspoon kosher salt

Freshly ground black pepper

½ cup / 85 g cooked and cooled farro
(see page 23)

⇥ Preheat the oven to 400°F.

⇥ Heat the olive oil in a 10-inch ovenproof skillet over medium heat. Add the shallot, asparagus, and fresh peas and cook, stirring occasionally, until the asparagus is just slightly tender yet still crisp, 4 to 5 minutes. The vegetables will continue to cook in the oven, so you're really just giving them a head start here. Season with a generous pinch of salt. (If using thawed frozen peas, stir them in now.) Remove from the heat.

↝ In a small bowl, whisk together the eggs, milk, cheese, salt, and a few grinds of pepper. Stir in the farro, then pour the mixture directly into the skillet, taking care to nudge the veggies around so they're evenly distributed throughout the frittata. (Since the pan is hot, the egg will start to immediately cook right around the edges.) Place the skillet in the oven and bake until the frittata is set, about 12 minutes. Loosen the edges of the frittata with the spatula and slice into wedges. Serve warm or at room temperature. Cover and refrigerate leftovers for up to 5 days.

Make It Your Own: *Use this recipe as a template and experiment with thinly sliced zucchini, leeks, mushrooms, sliced artichokes, or garlic scapes. If you can get ahold of a few fava beans, they're hearty and meaty and are wonderful folded in as well.*

California Barley Bowl *with* Lemony Yogurt Sauce

If you grew up in Northern California in the 1990s, you lived through the trend that was sprouts. From alfalfa sprouts to bean sprouts, they seemed to find their way into every green salad, sandwich, and omelet. This savory whole-grain breakfast bowl is inspired by those California days, with chunks of ripe avocado, crumbled Cotija cheese, toasty almonds, and a citrus-sparked yogurt sauce. While alfalfa sprouts were prevalent when I was growing up, today I try to branch out, using a tangle of colorful bean sprouts or more delicate radish or sunflower sprouts. These morning bowls couldn't be easier to prepare, but the barley does take a while to cook; I put a pot on the stove first thing in the morning so it'll be ready by the time I've had my coffee and prepped the other ingredients. Feel free to experiment with other grains, too. I've tried this with both quinoa and farro, and it's as wonderful with delicate grains as it is with heartier ones. SERVES 2, HEARTILY

Morning Notes: *Cotija cheese is popular in Mexican and Latin dishes. It's a firm, crumbly cheese made of cow's milk and is used so often because it's milder than feta or even goat cheese and softens with heat but doesn't fully melt. You can also use queso fresco if it's easier to find.*

1½ cups / 255 g cooked barley, still warm (see page 23)

1 cup / 55 g bean sprouts, any variety (I like mung bean sprouts)

⅓ cup / 60 g crumbled Cotija cheese or queso fresco

¼ cup / 20 g sliced almonds, toasted (see page 12)

¼ teaspoon kosher salt

1 small ripe avocado, peeled, pitted, and diced or sliced

Lemony Yogurt Sauce (page 72)

Flaky salt

Freshly ground black pepper

⤍ In a small bowl, stir the barley, sprouts, cheese, almonds, and kosher salt together. Scoop into 2 individual bowls and top with the avocado and a few generous spoonfuls of yogurt sauce. Sprinkle with flaky salt and pepper and serve.

Make Ahead: *Cooking the barley the night before is a great time-saver. Then these bowls really only take a few minutes to put together.*

Smoked Salmon Crème Fraîche Tart
with a Cornmeal Millet Crust

This savory tart is my number one excuse for picking up a little smoked salmon at the farmers' market. I fold it into a crème fraîche custard filling flecked with dill for a simple, versatile midday dish. Since you can enjoy the tart warm or at room temperature, it's also a fine contender for brunch, outdoor picnics, or morning potlucks. Whereas many savory tarts and quiches are weighed down with heavy cheeses, this recipe feels light and fluffy in comparison. It's great with a small green salad (I love including some bitter mustard greens), seasonal sliced fruit, or a simple cup of soup. SERVES 6 TO 8

Morning Notes: *If you can't find crème fraîche, it's easy to make your own at home (recipe follows), or substitute sour cream instead.*

CRUST

¹/₂ cup / 65 g fine-ground cornmeal

³/₄ cup / 90 g white whole wheat flour or standard whole wheat flour

³/₄ teaspoon kosher salt

6 tablespoons / 85 g cold unsalted butter, cut into ¹/₄-inch cubes, plus more for greasing the pan

3 to 4 tablespoons ice water

¹/₄ cup / 45 g millet

FILLING

1 tablespoon extra-virgin olive oil

¹/₂ cup / 50 g minced shallots (about 3 medium shallots)

2 cloves garlic, minced

1 cup / 240 ml whole milk

¹/₄ cup / 60 ml crème fraîche

3 large eggs, beaten

3 tablespoons capers, drained

2 tablespoons chopped fresh dill

1 teaspoon kosher salt

Pinch of freshly ground black pepper

4 ounces / 115 g smoked salmon, cut into small pieces

To prepare the crust: Butter a 9-inch tart pan with 1-inch sides and a removable bottom. Using a food processor fitted with the metal blade, pulse together the cornmeal, flour, and salt. Add the butter and pulse until the mixture resembles coarse meal (alternatively, you can use a pastry blender or your fingertips to work the butter into the dry ingredients). Add ice water 1 tablespoon at a time and pulse until the dough starts to look like wet, clumpy sand. It's ready if a small piece holds together when squeezed between your fingers. If it still seems too crumbly, add more water, 1 teaspoon at a time. Turn the

continued

dough out into a large bowl and mix in the millet using a fork. Press the dough evenly into the bottom and up the sides of the prepared pan. Chill in the refrigerator for at least 1 hour and up to 1 day.

⇥ Preheat the oven to 375°F. Place the prepared crust on a small baking sheet for easy transport to and from the oven.

⇥ Bake the crust for 15 minutes to slightly dry out the top so that it won't get soggy when you add the wet filling. Meanwhile, prepare the filling.

⇥ To prepare the filling: In a small sauté pan over medium heat, warm the olive oil and sauté the shallots until translucent, 2 to 3 minutes. Add the garlic and sauté for an additional 1 minute. Remove from the heat. In a bowl, whisk together the milk, crème fraîche, eggs, capers, dill, salt, and pepper to make a custard.

⇥ To assemble and bake the tart: Spoon the shallot mixture in an even layer on the bottom of the crust; arrange the salmon across the top evenly. Pour in the custard mixture.

⇥ Bake at 375°F until the top is golden brown and the filling is set, 30 to 35 minutes. Let cool for 15 to 20 minutes. Unmold the tart onto a serving platter and serve warm or at room temperature. If you have leftovers, cover and refrigerate for up to 3 days.

Make Ahead: *You can bake the crust a day ahead so the next day you simply whisk together the filling, pop the tart in the oven, and serve. If going this route, refrigerate the prebaked crust, covered with plastic wrap. You can also bake the entire tart up to 1 day in advance and allow it to cool, then refrigerate it, covered. To serve, reheat in a 300°F oven until warmed through, 12 to 15 minutes.*

Make Your Own Crème Fraîche: *Pour 2 tablespoons cultured buttermilk and 1 cup of unpasteurized or vat-pasteurized cream into a small glass jar. If your store only stocks ultra-pasteurized cream, it will still work—it'll just take much, much longer. Let the jar sit, uncovered, at room temperature for 12 to 36 hours. If you're worried about dust or other particles, cover loosely with a swath of cheesecloth. Once it firms up quite a bit, refrigerate for up to 2 weeks. The crème fraîche will continue to firm up in the refrigerator, so don't expect it to have your ultimate desired consistency right off the bat.*

Bacon *and* Kale Polenta Squares

Polenta certainly isn't as common as oatmeal or porridge for breakfast, but it's equally satisfying. Here, polenta is sliced and quickly panfried so the outside becomes slightly crispy while the inside stays pleasantly soft. SERVES 6 AS A LARGE PORTION, 9 AS A SMALLER PORTION

5 slices / 140 g thick-cut bacon

1¾ cups / 420 ml water, plus more if necessary

1 cup / 240 ml milk

¾ cup / 125 g polenta or stone-ground coarse cornmeal

1 teaspoon kosher salt

Freshly ground black pepper (optional)

½ bunch kale, stemmed and coarsely chopped (about 2½ cups / 125 g)

1 tablespoon extra-virgin olive oil

Flaky salt

⇥ Butter an 8-inch square baking pan. Line a plate with a few layers of paper towels.

⇥ In a medium skillet over medium-low heat, cook the bacon until crisp. Using tongs, transfer the bacon to the prepared plate to drain. Let the bacon cool enough to handle, then chop.

⇥ In a saucepan over medium-high heat, bring the water and milk to a gentle boil. Add the polenta and kosher salt and stir to combine. Decrease the heat to low. Simmer, uncovered, until the polenta is thick and creamy, 25 to 30 minutes, stirring often to prevent sticking or clumping. If it starts clumping or sticking to the bottom of the pan, add more water, 2 teaspoons at a time. Taste the polenta and adjust the seasoning as desired: I like to add a few grinds of pepper.

⇥ Add the kale and bacon and stir until the kale has wilted into the polenta, 1 to 2 minutes. Remove from the heat.

⇥ Scoop the hot polenta into the prepared baking dish and spread in an even layer. Refrigerate until firm, at least 1 hour. Slice the polenta into 6 large rectangles, or 9 smaller squares for side-dish portions.

⇥ In a nonstick pan over medium heat, warm the olive oil. Panfry the polenta squares on each side until golden brown and crispy, about 4 minutes per side. Finish with a few sprinkles of flaky salt.

Make It Your Own: *Experiment with other greens like Swiss chard or spinach. To make this vegetarian, omit the bacon and add cooked corn kernels, sautéed mushrooms, or sun-dried tomatoes.*

Make Ahead: *I think these squares are best eaten hot out of the skillet, but you certainly can make the polenta ahead of time and refrigerate it, covered, for up to 2 days before pan-frying.*

Strawberry Oat Breakfast Crisp

I've always found almonds and strawberries to be a natural marriage, and this recipe celebrates that. The nutty streusel topping is pleasantly schizophrenic. Halfway between a crisp and a cobbler, it features both almond meal and sliced almonds. I often serve this morning crisp with a scoop of thick yogurt. This is one of those dishes you set out for a gathering or a slow Sunday, and if you keep a spoon nearby, it disappears slowly, bite by bite. If the craving strikes in the dead of winter, feel free to make this recipe with frozen berries instead. SERVES 6 TO 8

TOPPING

$1\frac{1}{2}$ cups / 120 g sliced raw almonds

$\frac{1}{2}$ cup / 70 g whole wheat pastry flour

$\frac{1}{2}$ cup / 50 g rolled oats

2 teaspoons baking powder

$\frac{1}{2}$ teaspoon baking soda

3 tablespoons muscovado sugar or dark brown sugar

$\frac{1}{4}$ teaspoon kosher salt

$\frac{1}{4}$ teaspoon ground nutmeg

6 tablespoons / 85 g cold unsalted butter, cut into $\frac{1}{2}$-inch pieces, plus more for greasing the pan

$\frac{1}{4}$ cup / 60 ml buttermilk

FILLING

$1\frac{1}{2}$ pounds / 675 g strawberries, hulled and halved (about $4\frac{1}{2}$ cups / 1.1 L)

$\frac{1}{3}$ cup / 60 g natural cane sugar

1 tablespoon freshly squeezed lemon juice

1 teaspoon grated lemon zest

3 tablespoons cornstarch

⇥ Preheat the oven to 375°F. Butter an 11 by 7-inch baking dish.

⇥ To make the topping: Put 1 cup of the almonds in the bowl of a food processor fitted with the metal blade. Pulse for about 30 seconds, until you have a medium-fine almond meal. Add the flour, oats, baking powder, baking soda, muscovado sugar, salt, and nutmeg and pulse a few times to combine. Add the butter and pulse until the mixture resembles coarse cornmeal, about 30 seconds. Slowly add the buttermilk and continue pulsing until all of the liquid has been added. At this point, the dough should have come together and will look quite clumpy but not too wet. Transfer the dough to a mixing bowl and stir in the remaining $\frac{1}{2}$ cup sliced almonds. Place in the refrigerator while you prepare the filling.

❧ To prepare the filling: Toss together the strawberries, sugar, lemon juice, lemon zest, and cornstarch in a medium bowl. Scoop into the prepared baking dish.

❧ To assemble and bake the crisp: Pile the topping over the strawberries in an even layer and place in the oven. Bake until the top is golden brown and the juices are thickening and bubbling, 35 to 40 minutes. Remove from the oven and cool for at least 1 hour before serving. While I do think this crisp is best enjoyed the day it's made, if covered and stored at room temperature, it will keep for 1 additional day.

Make It Your Own: When rhubarb is in season, make a classic strawberry rhubarb crisp by swapping 2 cups of rhubarb for 2 cups of the strawberries. Cherries are another favorite and pair nicely with the almonds and oats.

Triple-Coconut Quinoa Porridge

Quinoa is an easy choice for a warm whole-grain cereal largely because it's so quick. While I often make this on busy weekdays because of the short ingredient list and minimal prep time, I also like to serve it as part of a brunch spread with a big bowl of seasonal fruit and something savory. It'll take you less than half an hour, but this porridge comes across as special—even a touch dressy—thanks to the three kinds of coconut (coconut milk, coconut flakes, and a drizzle of melted coconut oil on top). It's slightly creamy, fragrant, and only mildly sweet. SERVES 4 TO 6

Morning Notes: *If you'd prefer to use low-fat coconut milk, it makes the porridge a bit lighter and not quite as decadent, but no less delightful. While the coconut oil on top is optional, it's quite delicious, so I do hope you do try it.*

1¼ cups / 60 g unsweetened
coconut flakes

1 vanilla bean, split, or 1 teaspoon
pure vanilla extract

1 cup / 180 g quinoa, rinsed

1 (13.5-ounce / 400 ml) can
unsweetened coconut milk

¼ cup / 60 ml water

2 tablespoons natural cane sugar,
plus more for serving

¼ teaspoon ground ginger

¼ teaspoon kosher salt

1 to 2 tablespoons melted coconut oil,
for serving (optional)

⇥ Preheat the oven to 325°F.

⇥ Put ¾ cup of the coconut flakes in a small baking dish and toast in the oven until fragrant and just golden brown, 5 to 7 minutes. Set aside.

⇥ Scrape the vanilla seeds into a heavy-bottomed pot. Add the vanilla pod, quinoa, coconut milk, water, sugar, ginger, salt, and remaining ½ cup of the coconut flakes and stir to combine. Over medium heat, bring the mixture to a slow boil. Decrease the heat to low and cover the pot. Cook until most of the liquid has been absorbed, stirring a few times to avoid sticking, 18 to 20 minutes. Remove the vanilla pod.

⇥ Remove from the heat and let sit for 10 minutes, covered. Spoon into bowls and garnish with the toasted coconut flakes, a sprinkle of sugar, and a drizzle of the melted coconut oil.

Make Ahead: *This porridge keeps for up to 3 days in the refrigerator and can easily be made in advance. If doing so, you may need to add a few teaspoons of water to reheat on the stovetop or in the microwave. Don't pour on the melted coconut oil until ready to serve.*

A BOOMING BUSINESS

In May 2012, the *Wall Street Journal* called. They told me they needed me to overnight Marge Granola to their New York office for a photo shoot. In one sense, this wasn't a complete surprise. I'd been speaking on and off with one of the food writers for months after she'd ordered granola online and fallen in love with it. Then, when we redesigned the granola packaging and launched two new flavors, she felt like the time was right for a small profile of the company. I called my parents. I ordered extra oats—five hundred pounds of extra oats, to be exact. I had the Vermont farm that ships my maple syrup on call. I felt ready.

Saturday morning as I drove to pick up the newspaper, I casually pulled out my phone to see if anyone might have placed an order. My email had exploded overnight. There were dozens upon dozens of orders, seemingly coming in every few seconds. As the hours ticked on, I grew worried. This was a whole lot of granola. Sam started making a spreadsheet. I started pacing.

The coming weeks brought little sleep and lots of oats. The business has never been the same. In addition to all the orders, that small chunk of time last summer encouraged immediate lessons in shipping, streamlining my ordering process, and hiring. It was all a lesson in quick scaling up, and for the first time, I felt like Marge Granola had a future that I could actually envision. A future beyond my little blue tablecloth-covered farmers' market booth. A future that involved Sam, my sister (and first employee) Rachael, and me baking, packaging, writing, designing, and dreaming of the next iteration.

Strawberry Rhubarb Quick Jam

I went through a very brief jam-making period the spring I lived in San Francisco. It faded quickly because I'm just not one for sterilizing jars or fussing with thermometers. So you can imagine that my discovery of quick jam changed everything. Because this recipe doesn't contain pectin, it will be a little looser than traditional store-bought jams—all the better to stir it into anything you can get your hands on (yogurt, porridge, even vanilla ice cream). The lemon brightens the whole thing so it actually feels like summer might just be on the horizon, even if you happen to be in foggy San Francisco. MAKES ABOUT 2½ CUPS

2 cups / 230 g chopped rhubarb
(approximately 4 medium stalks)

1 pound / 450 g fresh strawberries,
hulled and chopped (about 3 cups /
720 ml)

1¼ cups / 230 g natural cane sugar
or granulated white sugar

Pinch of kosher salt

2 teaspoons freshly squeezed
lemon juice

1 teaspoon grated lemon zest

⇥ In a large bowl, stir the rhubarb, strawberries, and sugar together and let them macerate until the sugar has begun to dissolve into the fruit, about 10 minutes. Transfer to a heavy-bottomed pot. Bring to a boil over medium heat. Stir in the salt, lemon juice, and lemon zest and decrease the heat to medium-low.

⇥ Gently simmer until the fruit breaks down and the mixture starts to cook down, diminishing in size by about one-third and thickening slightly, 15 to 20 minutes. Stir occasionally to avoid sticking. If the fruit isn't breaking down on its own, use the back of a wooden spoon or a potato masher to help it out (I tend to like a chunkier jam, so I don't go to great lengths to do this). Skim off any foam that may congregate at the top.

⇥ Ideally, when the jam is close to being done, the mixture will still be loose (it'll firm up more as it cools) but should coat the back of a wooden spoon. Remove from the heat and pour into a bowl to fully stop the cooking process. Let it cool completely. Transfer to clean glass jars and store in the refrigerator for up to 3 weeks, or in the freezer for up to 6 months.

Freezer Tips: *I don't generally freeze this jam because we end up going through it easily in 3 weeks. When I do freeze it, I use an airtight plastic container, but if you decide to store the jam in glass jars, don't use a jar with curved sides; reach for widemouthed, straight-sided jars only. When you freeze a liquid jam, it will expand a smidge inside the jar and can press against any curves, resulting in a messy, jam-filled freezer.*

Lemony Yogurt Sauce

This bright, creamy yogurt sauce is lightly flecked with herbs and is great for everything from drizzling over savory bowls of grains to spooning on top of fried rice, breakfast hash, or Buckwheat Crepes (page 118). Double the recipe for a larger group or to keep a little jar of the sauce in the refrigerator. It's season-less, really. SERVES 2

Morning Notes: *Depending on the kind of yogurt you use and how you prefer the consistency of this sauce, feel free to add a spoonful (or two) of cold water to thin it out.*

½ cup / 120 ml plain yogurt (a runnier, non-Greek yogurt works best), homemade (page 25) or store-bought

1 teaspoon grated lemon zest

1 teaspoon freshly squeezed lemon juice

1 tablespoon chopped fresh chives

Pinch of kosher salt

Whisk all the ingredients together in a small bowl. Refrigerate any leftovers in an airtight container for up to 3 days. If the sauce begins to separate, just give it a good stir before using.

Green Herb Sauce

Most of us are accustomed to jams, compotes, and conserves in the mornings, so an herb sauce may seem an odd choice at the breakfast table. But with savory recipes, I love a dollop of this vibrant bright spread, and I keep a little jar in the refrigerator regardless of the season. It does wonders to wake up warm leftover grains, soft-scrambled eggs, or Cheesy Chive Millet Grits (page 54). Inspired by a walnut pesto from Andrew Weil's book *The Healthy Kitchen*, this version differs with the addition of lemon, fresh parsley, and dill.

MAKES ABOUT 1 CUP

¾ cup / 75 g walnuts, toasted (see page 12) and cooled

1 cup / 25 g chopped fresh cilantro

1 cup / 25 g chopped fresh flat-leaf parsley

1 tablespoon chopped fresh dill

2 cloves garlic

1 tablespoon coarsely chopped shallot

Generous pinch of kosher salt

2 tablespoons freshly squeezed lemon juice

3 tablespoons extra-virgin olive oil

Cold water, as needed, for thinning the sauce

⇥ Put the walnuts in a food processor fitted with the metal blade and process until fine. Add the cilantro, parsley, dill, garlic, shallot, salt, lemon juice, and olive oil. Process until smooth. The sauce should be the consistency of a thick pesto. If it's too thick, add water, 1 teaspoon at a time, to get a spoonable consistency that you're happy with. Refrigerate any leftovers in an airtight container for up to 7 days. You'll likely need to give the stored sauce a good stir before using it.

SUMMER
settling in

A FUNNY THING HAPPENS AROUND AUGUST. While I'm surrounded by beautiful produce, berries, and stone fruit, I always fumble around in the kitchen as if I've never prepared a meal before. Yogurt and a handful of blueberries are a typical breakfast. Sliced ripe tomatoes with salt and a crusty baguette: dinner. At the height of Seattle's summer, it stays light until 10 p.m., so we find ourselves cobbling together a dinner to eat in the backyard or moseying over to a friend's restaurant late in the evening.

The first summer I lived in Seattle, there were a few months of settling in. I guess people call this nesting. Sam and I unpacked during the rainy spring and then began to stretch our limbs and claim our new neighborhood in early summer. The coffee shop a block away has come to double as our office, I can walk to the post office and the bank, and our local bar has a great selection of dark beers and warm, salty tortilla chips. During those months of nesting and exploring, we'd run down to the beach or walk the neighbor-hood alleys, peeking over fences at the sweet craftsman houses and gardens. It felt like home in no time.

Initially, we had our fair share of tiptoeing around each other, discovering shared rituals and traditions. I learned how Sam likes to reuse his loose tea to make numerous cups throughout the day and washes plastic bags and aluminum foil to reuse them for the umpteenth time. I began calling him my "Depression-era boyfriend" and hid my Swiffers and paper towels so as to avoid discussions on environmentally wasteful cleaning prod-ucts. We took stock of our collective appliances and kitchen equipment and donated a few things (no house needs two salad spinners). But for the most part, we've kept what was uniquely ours. Two espresso machines sit proudly on the counter. Mine, a brand new model—squatty and colorful, quick and without mess. It makes a shot of espresso that's uniform and tasty, but never spectacular. Sam's, a contraption that calls for a good deal of time and a little fuss before offering up a shot of espresso that's a true thing of beauty. In this way, we not only joined our espresso machines, our two rather well-stocked bars, and our large book collections, but we also joined our established quirks. This says a lot about our house and about us, really—two very different approaches to things that coexist just fine. Happily so, in fact.

Beyond our own kitchen, my first summer in Seattle brought about many lessons on how the region's produce differed from what I was used to in the Bay Area. I discovered gooseberries, red and white currants, and huckleberries. Sweet and sour cherries were easier to come by, wild blackberries grew along my running route, and native berries like salal and Saskatoon berries popped up at farmers' markets. When Sam promised that if I moved north, I'd see it really was paradise, he was right, at least on this count. You put in your time with the darker winter and spring months and then summer comes, beckoning you outside with long days, wild berries, a regular bounty, and a picnic table for two.

SEASONAL *Spotlight*

Summer is the season for stone fruits, berries, and tomatoes. For this reason alone, it's a really good time of year. **Peaches** and **nectarines** get juicier as they ripen; choose fruits that are fragrant with slightly soft but not mushy (or hard) flesh. Berries make a formidable showing, with the little blue baskets taking over our kitchen counter come August. A good tip is to only rinse your berries right before using them to avoid mold and spoilage. Look for **cherries** with stems intact; each year I debate whether the dark maroon Bings or the more mottled red and yellow Rainiers are sweeter. The jury's still out. **Raspberries** are a delicate, juicy berry—wonderful paired with cream, honey, and cocoa. Tart **blackberries** and sweet **blueberries** invite pies, muffins, and jams.

Tomatoes are a favorite summer treat. In the Bay Area, I bought bags of dry-farmed Early Girl tomatoes. Here in Seattle, I quickly discovered the sweet Mountain Magic variety. Look for fragrant tomatoes that are slightly soft to the touch, and store them at room temperature, as refrigerating dulls the flavor dramatically. Ears of **sweet corn** are most commonly found in yellow and white varieties. A good ear of corn has nice green husks that wrap around the kernels snugly; make sure to refrigerate corn with the husk intact for longer life (three to four days) and better flavor. **Fresh herbs** are a star of summer cooking. From basil to thyme to parsley, I toss chopped herbs into savory grain bowls, quiches, morning tarts, and egg dishes.

Vanilla *and* Cream
Steel-Cut Oats Porridge

In these days of instant oatmeal and on-the-go breakfasts, I find steel-cut oats a breath of fresh air, even if they take a few extra minutes in the morning. I started making this breakfast at my mom's cabin in the Adirondacks, where the days are long and the itineraries short, so finding extra time in the morning was never an issue. I top my oats with a little cream because my grandmother loves them that way, and I've learned to love it as well.

SERVES 4

Morning Notes: *Steel-cut oats take longer to cook than rolled oats, but they're chewier and almost creamy, and cooking them in a mixture of water and whole milk makes them even creamier. There are a few tricks to cooking them well: toasting your oats first will draw out their warm, nutty flavor, and adding the toasted oats to already-hot liquid (versus heating them all up in the same pot together) will ensure they remain toothsome and delicious.*

1 tablespoon unsalted butter

1 cup / 175 g steel-cut oats

3 ¼ cups / 780 ml water

1 cup / 240 ml milk

1 tablespoon natural cane sugar

½ teaspoon kosher salt

¾ cup / 105 g raisins

1 ¼ teaspoons pure vanilla extract

Brown sugar, honey, or maple syrup, for serving (optional)

Heavy cream, for serving (optional)

In a heavy-bottomed skillet, melt the butter over medium heat. Add the oats and stir and toss gently in the pan until quite fragrant, 5 to 6 minutes; set aside.

In a saucepan, bring the water, milk, sugar, and salt to a low simmer over medium heat. Stir in the toasted oats. Bring to a slow boil, decrease the heat to low, and partially cover. Cook the porridge, stirring occasionally to avoid sticking or clumping, until it has thickened and the oats have softened, 25 to 30 minutes. The porridge will still be a little loose at this point, but don't worry; it will continue to soak up additional liquid.

Stir in the raisins and vanilla and cover. Remove from the heat and let sit for 3 to 5 minutes to allow the raisins to plump and soften.

Scoop into serving bowls and top with brown sugar, honey, or maple syrup and a splash of cream.

Make It Your Own: *I usually stick with brown sugar and honey as toppings, but feel free to use any nuts and spices that you may like. For inspiration, see Toppings and Stir-Ins, page 44.*

Yogurt Cups *with* Roasted Black Cherries *and* Toasted Millet

These yogurt cups are in constant rotation during the height of cherry season because of their dreamy combination of flavors and textures: crunchy millet, plump cherries, and creamy yogurt. To serve, I use my favorite little bowls or oversized teacups instead of parfait glasses or glass jars. I love stirring the cherries and their juices right into the yogurt and scattering the millet throughout rather than neatly layering everything. In this case, messy rules! You can vary this recipe seasonally by using any fresh fruit you like instead of roasted cherries. Strawberries and sliced mango are another favorite. SERVES 4

Morning Notes: If you want to make your own yogurt, it is an overnight process, so plan accordingly. And about yogurt: while I certainly like Greek yogurt, a looser European-style yogurt is really nice here as it allows the cherries and millet to happily mingle.

¾ cup / 135 g millet

3 cups / 720 ml plain yogurt, homemade (page 25) or store-bought

1½ cups / 360 ml Roasted Black Cherries (page 99)

2 tablespoons honey (optional)

⇥ To toast the millet: Pour the millet into a large, dry skillet over medium heat. Toast until fragrant, 4 to 6 minutes, stirring occasionally so it doesn't burn or stick to the pan. As it toasts, the millet will pop and jump a little. Remove from the heat and set aside to cool.

⇥ To assemble the cups: Spoon ½ cup of the yogurt into the bottom of each cup. Sprinkle each with 1 tablespoon of the toasted millet and top with a large spoonful of roasted cherries (get a little of the juice in there if you can). Top each with ¼ cup of the yogurt and another generous spoonful of cherries. Finish each with about 2 tablespoons of toasted millet and a generous teaspoonful of honey if you'd like. These are best enjoyed shortly after they're made.

Make Ahead: Feel free to make all of the components ahead of time (roast the cherries, toast the millet, and make your homemade yogurt). Just wait to put them all together in serving bowls until the morning to prevent the millet from getting soggy and the cherries from getting limp.

Quick Breakfast Fried Rice

If you're not accustomed to eating fried rice for breakfast, we obviously didn't live in the same college dorm. I love this grown-up version because there are still those mornings when you stare into the refrigerator and have difficulty imagining how all the little bowls of leftovers might somehow come together into a meal. Breakfast rice is almost always the answer. All you need: leftover rice, a few eggs, a little bacon if you'd like, and a couple of green onions. Ginger, lemon, and parsley complete this most crave-worthy morning meal. SERVES 4

Morning Notes: *While I prefer slightly fragrant and nutritious long-grain brown rice, use any leftover rice you have on hand—or really, any leftover grains at all.*

4 ounces / 115 g thick-cut bacon, chopped

4 tablespoons / 60 ml sesame oil

3 green onions, white and light green parts, finely chopped (about 3 tablespoons)

2 cloves garlic, minced

4 large eggs

3 cups / 400 g day-old cooked long-grain brown rice, at room temperature (see page 23)

1 tablespoon minced fresh ginger

3 tablespoons sesame seeds, toasted (see page 12), plus more for serving

2 tablespoons low-sodium soy sauce

1 tablespoon grated lemon zest

Kosher salt (optional)

Freshly ground black pepper (optional)

⅓ cup / 7 g chopped fresh flat-leaf parsley (optional)

In a large heavy-bottomed skillet, cook the bacon over medium heat until brown and crisp, 5 to 7 minutes. Use a slotted spoon to transfer the bacon to a plate lined with paper towels to drain. Drain the bacon drippings from the skillet.

Place the skillet back on stove over medium heat and pour in 3 tablespoons of the sesame oil. Add the green onions and garlic and sauté until fragrant, 1 to 2 minutes. Decrease the heat to low, break the eggs directly into the skillet, and scramble them. Add the rice, bacon, ginger, remaining 1 tablespoon of sesame oil, sesame seeds, soy sauce, and lemon zest. Stir to combine and cook until warmed throughout. Taste and season with salt and pepper if desired. Stir in the parsley at the very end.

Scoop into bowls and sprinkle with toasted sesame seeds. Serve hot.

Make It Your Own: *If I have leftover chicken or pulled pork, I often omit the bacon and stir bits of that in toward the end. Alternatively, make this a vegetarian recipe by omitting the bacon altogether. If you'd like to dress it up a bit, fold in a few diced sautéed vegetables like squash, zucchini, or carrots and top with a dash of hot sauce—if that's your kind of thing.*

Dried Cherry, Almond, and Flax Muesli

In the warmer months, I find myself reaching for muesli and yogurt for quick weekday breakfasts. It has all of the wonderful nuts and seeds that granola has without the extra sugar or oil. So I experiment with muesli a lot, adding dibs and dabs of whatever I have on hand in the pantry at any given time. In that way, this recipe is very much a template for a DIY muesli: use any nuts and seeds you like and experiment with different dried fruits. While you can enjoy muesli much like you would granola, with milk or yogurt, it's wonderful soaked overnight, too. MAKES ABOUT 5 CUPS

Morning Notes: *This muesli is delicious raw (as offered here), but if you'd prefer to toast the nuts and seeds first, it adds a special crunch and depth of flavor that can be nice if you have a few extra minutes in the morning. See Toasting Nuts, page 11.*

3 cups / 300 g rolled oats

¼ cup / 15 g wheat bran or oat bran

¾ cup / 60 g sliced raw almonds

¼ cup / 30 g raw sunflower seeds

3 tablespoons flaxseeds

½ cup / 70 g dried cherries, chopped

¼ teaspoon kosher salt

¼ teaspoon ground ginger

Plain yogurt, kefir, milk, nut milk, or apple juice, for serving

Honey or jam, for serving (optional)

In a large bowl, combine the oats, bran, almonds, sunflower seeds, flaxseeds, dried cherries, salt, and ginger. Transfer to a large jar and enjoy as you would granola or any other cereal, adding yogurt, milk, or nut milk as you please.

Alternatively, soak your muesli overnight: For a single serving, scoop out ¾ cup muesli and stir it into ½ cup yogurt or kefir and ¼ cup milk or apple juice. Let sit in the refrigerator overnight, or at least 3 hours. In the morning, remove the muesli from the fridge and let come to room temperature, 10 to 15 minutes. Add an extra splash of milk if you like your muesli a bit looser (I do) and a dollop of honey or your favorite jam.

MUESLI:
To Soak or Not to Soak

Medical experts and nutritionists have a lot to say about soaking grains, something many ancient populations did before eating them. Often if a recipe calls for soaking grains overnight, it's meant to speed up the cooking process or to boost our body's ability to absorb the nutrients. Soaking muesli for at least twelve hours *does* soften the oats and is supposed to help with digestion and nutrient absorption. But I usually just plain forget or am simply not thinking through the next day's meals a day in advance. Nutritional theories change with trends and new evidence, so I always like to balance that information with my own instincts and lifestyle. And for that reason, I don't always soak my muesli overnight.

That being said, there are times when soaking muesli overnight just makes good sense. My mom's cabin in Upstate New York is an old, turn-of-the-century camp on Lake George that can be quite restful and wonderful, but when packed in the summer with family of all ages, boyfriends, pets, and various electronic devices, it becomes loud, cramped, and hot. Really hot. So there's nothing better on those sticky mornings than to wake up to a cool, milky bowl of soft, fruity muesli. I do make the effort to soak muesli in the summer—it's my reward for a night of mosquitoes and still, still air.

Many people I know use milk or nut milk to soak their muesli, but I usually use thinned yogurt because I like the tanginess of it, and because it feels a little more substantial that way. If you're in a hurry, you can even soak your muesli for 30 minutes before rushing out the door, or add it to a small mason jar with milk or nut milk and take it on the go to enjoy midmorning at work.

Try muesli both ways and decide when to make the effort. And know to turn the other way when your family members scoff just a little at your choice of "milky mush" over bacon. Or maybe you'll just have a little of both, like I do.

Easy Gruyère Soufflés *with* Fresh Corn, Leeks, *and* Millet

I rarely make breakfast soufflés at home because the necessary separating of eggs and proper whipping seem too complex in the morning. But this recipe is refreshingly simple: the herb-flecked eggs are poured right over the vegetable and grain mixture, and the soufflés puff up into delightful golden mounds in the oven. No separating or whipping or fuss. If you're new to millet, this is a great introduction because its mild corn flavor and pleasing texture blend right into the savory egg custard. Best served warm right out of the oven. Newspaper and dark coffee optional. SERVES 4

Morning Notes: *While I love the look of these soufflés in ramekins, you can prepare them in a standard muffin tin as well (instructions follow the main recipe).*

½ cup / 90 g millet

1 cup / 240 ml water

2 tablespoons extra-virgin olive oil

1 medium leek, rinsed well, white and light green parts, diced (1¼ cups / 95 g)

1¼ cups / 190 g fresh corn kernels (cut from 2 small ears) or frozen corn kernels, thawed

2 cloves garlic, minced

1 tablespoon unsalted butter, for greasing the ramekins

6 large eggs

¾ cup / 180 ml whole milk

1 teaspoon dried basil

1 teaspoon dried chives

¼ teaspoon kosher salt

¼ teaspoon red pepper flakes

¾ cup / 70 g shredded Gruyère cheese

Flaky salt (optional)

Preheat the oven to 400°F. Thoroughly butter four 10-ounce ramekins. Place the ramekins on a baking sheet so they'll move easily to and from the oven.

Put the millet and a generous pinch of salt in a small saucepan. Pour in the water and bring to a boil. Decrease the heat to medium-low and cook for 10 minutes. Drain off any excess liquid and set the millet aside. It won't be fully cooked at this point, but it will finish cooking as the soufflés bake.

In a medium saucepan, warm the olive oil over medium heat. Add the leek and fresh corn, if using, and sauté until the leek is soft and translucent, 5 to 7 minutes (if using frozen corn, fold it in at the very end). Add the garlic and sauté for an additional 1 to 2 minutes, taking care not to let it brown or burn. Add the millet and stir to combine. If using thawed frozen corn, fold it in at this time. Set aside.

In a small bowl, whisk together the eggs, milk, basil, chives, kosher salt, and red pepper flakes. Fold in the cheese. Scoop ½ cup of the corn mixture into the bottom of each ramekin, then pour the milk mixture over the top, filling each ramekin. The cheese can clump up, so try to be sure it's distributed among all 4 ramekins evenly.

Bake until the tops are golden and have puffed slightly, 20 to 25 minutes. Sprinkle with flaky salt if you'd like. Serve warm. Cover and refrigerate any leftovers for up to 3 days.

Make It Your Own: *To bake in muffin tins, butter each muffin cup liberally. Follow the ingredient preparation instructions in the main recipe. Scoop ¼ cup of the corn mixture into each muffin cup and fill just to the brim with the milk mixture. Bake until the tops are golden and they've puffed and raised like muffins, 18 to 20 minutes.*

ON MORNING EGGS

I find that if we have a few eggs, a bit of cheese, and some leftover grains, we always have a morning meal at the ready. From softly scrambled with fresh herbs and a little chèvre to folded into seasonal vegetables and grains for a frittata or omelet, eggs are one of the mainstays of our breakfasts, especially on the weekends. Eggs contain all nine essential amino acids and a handful of vitamins, and they keep me satisfied and energized through midday with their punch of protein. Below you'll find a couple of my favorite ways to prepare them.

How to Softly Fry an Egg

In a heavy-bottomed nonstick pan large enough to hold 3 or 4 large eggs (I like a 12-inch skillet here), heat 2 tablespoons of extra-virgin olive oil over medium heat until shimmering. Swirl to coat the pan. If you're new to frying eggs, perhaps just do 1 or 2 eggs at a time until you get the hang of it. Gently crack the eggs into the pan, leaving enough space around each so they don't stick to one another. For sunny-side up eggs (cooked only on one side), cook until the whites are just set and the yolk is slightly firm but still runny, 3 to 4 minutes. If you like your eggs over easy, flip them at the point where the egg whites are set but the yolk is still soft. Then cook on the second side for an additional 30 seconds or so. Sprinkle with flaky salt and pepper.

How to Poach an Egg

Fill a small saucepan halfway with water and heat to the point where it's almost simmering; don't let it come to a full boil. Add a few teaspoons of distilled white vinegar to the water. Crack an egg gently into a small teacup or ramekin. Gently tip the egg into the water and poach for about 4 minutes. As it's poaching, you can very carefully guide the egg white toward the center of the egg with a wooden spoon for a rounder, prettier egg. If you don't, it will still taste wonderful—it will just be a touch shaggy. Remove the egg with a slotted spoon.

Zucchini Farro Cakes, Two Ways

These whole-grain zucchini cakes can be reheated and topped with a simple fried egg on an average Wednesday or cooked to order on a slow Sunday and topped with creamy goat cheese and slow-roasted ripe tomatoes. If you've made latkes or panfried fritters at home, you know that forming the patties can be a bit haphazard. That's the beauty of this recipe: when so much in our day-to-day life needs neatening, these savory cakes decidedly do not. MAKES 10 TO 12 CAKES

Morning Notes: A piece of inexpensive cheesecloth will make draining the zucchini a cinch (see Sources, page 166). Also, feel free to experiment with different hearty grains, like wheat berries, spelt berries, rye berries, or barley. Avoid small, more delicate grains like quinoa or amaranth.

3 ½ cups / 430 g shredded zucchini (about 1 pound / 450 g or 3 medium)

1 teaspoon kosher salt

2 cups / 340 g cooked and cooled farro (see page 23)

3 large eggs, beaten

3 green onions, white and light green parts, finely chopped (about 3 tablespoons)

3 tablespoons chopped fresh flat-leaf parsley

1 tablespoon chopped fresh thyme

1 cup / 125 g bread crumbs

2 tablespoons white whole wheat flour or standard whole wheat flour

2 cloves garlic, minced

2 tablespoons extra-virgin olive oil, plus more if needed

In a bowl, toss the zucchini with ½ teaspoon of the salt and set aside for 8 to 10 minutes. Drain by squeezing the zucchini in cheesecloth or a fine-weave kitchen towel. When finished, you should be left with about 1½ cups of relatively dry shredded zucchini.

In a large bowl, combine the farro, eggs, remaining ½ teaspoon salt, green onions, parsley, thyme, bread crumbs, flour, garlic, and zucchini. Stir well and let stand for 5 minutes. Knead the mixture a few times in the bowl with your hands, then form 3-inch patties, about ¾ inch thick, and place them on a plate to await cooking.

Line a large plate with paper towels. Pour the olive oil into a large heavy-bottomed skillet over medium heat. Once the oil is hot and almost shimmering, put 4 of the patties in the pan and cook until the bottom is golden brown, about 4 minutes. Flip and cook the second side for 3 to 4 minutes. Place the cooked cakes on the lined plate to drain off any excess oil. Repeat with the remaining patties, adding a little extra oil as needed between batches if the cakes begin to stick to the pan.

Following are two of my favorite ways to serve these cakes.

continued

Zucchini Farro Cakes Topped with a Quick Fried Egg

To make these on a weekday, prepare the batter the night before and refrigerate. Or cook all of the cakes in advance (see Make Ahead, following) and simply reheat. Stack 1 or 2 warm cakes on each plate and top with a fried egg (see page 86).

Zucchini Farro Cakes with Herbed Goat Cheese and Slow-Roasted Tomatoes

If you'd rather use heirloom or Roma tomatoes in lieu of cherry tomatoes, go right ahead. Cut them in ½-inch slices and keep an eye on them, as they tend to cook more quickly. To save time, prepare the goat cheese and roast the tomatoes up to 3 days in advance; store them, covered, in the refrigerator until you're ready to cook the zucchini cakes and serve.

SLOW-ROASTED TOMATOES
1 pound / 450 g (about 2¼ cups / 540 ml)
   cherry tomatoes
3 tablespoons extra-virgin olive oil
¼ teaspoon kosher salt
A few grinds of black pepper

HERBED GOAT CHEESE
5 ounces / 140 g soft goat cheese
2 teaspoons chopped fresh chives
1 teaspoon chopped fresh dill
1 teaspoon chopped fresh tarragon
A few grinds of black pepper
3 tablespoons milk

To roast the tomatoes: Preheat the oven to 250°F. Line a baking sheet with parchment paper.

Arrange the tomatoes on the prepared baking sheet. Drizzle with the olive oil so each tomato is covered nicely, and sprinkle with the salt and pepper. Bake until the tomatoes become shriveled, a bit browned on the edges, and incredibly soft and juicy, about 3 hours. Stir every hour or so to ensure they're still covered in olive oil.

To prepare the goat cheese: Put the cheese, chives, dill, tarragon, and pepper in a small bowl and use the back of a spoon to mash the herbs into the cheese. Add the milk and stir vigorously to soften the cheese.

To assemble: Serve warm or at room temperature. Top each cake with a generous dollop of herbed goat cheese and a spoonful of juicy roasted tomatoes.

Make Ahead: *To save time, you can make the zucchini mix or form the cakes up to 1 day in advance; keep them covered in the refrigerator overnight. You can also bake the cakes, allow them to cool, and refrigerate them for up to 4 to 5 days. To reheat, warm in a 250°F oven or in the microwave on high heat for 45 seconds to 1 minute, until warmed through.*

Caramelized Nectarines *with* Honeyed Ricotta *and* Quinoa Crunch

This pretty breakfast is deceptive, as it looks time-consuming but is really quite simple. While I love fruit-rich breakfasts, especially in the spring and summer, my body also craves protein in the morning. This recipe is the perfect solution because quinoa is such a high-protein grain, and ricotta has its fair share, too. You can substitute peaches for nectarines if that's what you have on hand. SERVES 4 TO 6

Morning Notes: *If you have a cast-iron pan, this is the time to break it out—it will leave a beautiful char on the delicate nectarines.*

2 tablespoons extra-virgin olive oil

2 tablespoons honey

4 ripe nectarines (about 1¼ pounds / 565 g), halved and pitted

1 tablespoon freshly squeezed orange juice

Honeyed Ricotta (page 131), for serving

Quinoa Crunch (page 43), for serving

Heat the olive oil in a 10- or 12-inch skillet over medium-high heat. When the oil is shimmering hot, add the honey and stir to combine. Put the nectarines, cut-side down, in the pan. Decrease the heat to medium and cook until the bottoms begin to brown and the flesh softens, 8 to 10 minutes, scooting the fruit halves around in the pan periodically to ensure they're not sticking. During this time, the honey will bubble up and darken. Decrease the heat to low and add the orange juice. Swirl the pan to distribute the juices evenly. Gently flip the nectarines. Continue cooking for 5 minutes, then remove from the heat.

To serve, place one nectarine half on each plate, spoon a large dollop of Honeyed Ricotta on each, and generously sprinkle with Quinoa Crunch. Serve immediately.

Make It Your Own: *I love the flavor of nectarines and rosemary together, so for a slightly savory touch, add 1 tablespoon fresh rosemary when you add the orange juice to the pan—it will soften into the warm, sweet honey.*

Rosemary Apricot Oatcakes

There's a wonderful salt shop in Portland, Oregon, called The Meadows. They stock a flaky rosemary finishing salt that I sprinkle on top of these oatcakes, which only have a kiss of sweetness and bake up a touch crumbly and quite substantial—almost biscuity in nature. I make oatcakes often because of their relatively long shelf life; it's nice to have something around the house to grab and take to my desk first thing in the morning when there isn't time for a proper breakfast. In lieu of apricots, chopped dates or rehydrated dried figs are both tried-and-true winners. MAKES 12 TO 15

Morning Notes: *Quinoa flakes add nice texture and a bit of chew, but if you have trouble finding them, substitute additional rolled oats instead.*

¾ cup / 75 g rolled oats

½ cup / 40 g quinoa flakes

¼ cup / 60 ml warm water

1 cup / 120 g white whole wheat flour

2 tablespoons natural cane sugar

½ teaspoon baking soda

1 teaspoon baking powder

¼ cup / 30 g raw sesame seeds

½ teaspoon kosher salt

¼ teaspoon freshly ground black pepper

2½ teaspoons dried rosemary

½ cup / 30 g shredded Parmesan cheese

½ cup / 75 g finely chopped dried apricots (about 10 dried apricots)

8 tablespoons / 115 g unsalted butter

2 tablespoons honey

1 large egg, beaten

Flaky salt

⇥ Preheat the oven to 350°F. Line 2 baking sheets with parchment paper or a silicone mat.

⇥ Put the oats and quinoa flakes in a small bowl and add the warm water. Mix with a fork to incorporate.

⇥ In a medium bowl, combine the flour, sugar, baking soda, baking powder, sesame seeds, kosher salt, pepper, rosemary, Parmesan, and apricots. Add the oat mixture and stir to combine.

⇥ In a small saucepan, heat the butter and honey over medium heat, stirring often, until warm and combined. Pour over the dry ingredients. Add the egg and mix well.

⇥ Scoop out about 2 or 3 tablespoons of dough and form into a ball. The smaller size of the oatcakes helps hold their shape better. Place on the lined baking sheets, spacing them about 1½ inches apart. Using the palm of your hand, gently flatten the cookies until they're about ¼ inch thick. Sprinkle each with a tiny pinch of flaky salt.

⇥ Bake until golden brown around the edges, about 15 minutes. Let cool at least 10 minutes on the baking sheet before serving. If kept in an airtight container at room temperature, these cookies will remain fresh for 5 to 6 days.

Peach Breakfast Cobbler *with* Cornmeal Thyme Biscuits

The fragrance released by juicy peaches baking beneath herbed-cornmeal biscuits is a very fine thing to wake up to on a summer Sunday morning. Because this cobbler takes a little time to bake, I'll mix the dry ingredients for the biscuits the night before. When I wake up, I'm just slicing peaches and adding the wet ingredients to the dough while the coffee is brewing. By the time I've finished my first cup of coffee, it's ready to pull from the oven. For added decadence, serve with a dollop of Greek yogurt, crème fraîche, or Honeyed Ricotta (page 131). I use my ten-inch cast-iron skillet here, but if you don't have one at home, feel free to make this in a two-quart baking dish instead. SERVES 6

Morning Notes: I don't peel peaches for this recipe. They soften and cook down just fine, so you'll hardly notice the skins. If you're set on doing so, cut a small X with a paring knife on the bottom of each peach, then dunk the peaches in almost boiling water for 60 seconds or so; the skins will slide right off.

FILLING

2 pounds / 900 g ripe peaches, pitted and halved (5 to 6 peaches)

¼ cup / 45 g natural cane sugar

2 tablespoons freshly squeezed lemon juice

1 teaspoon grated lemon zest

3 tablespoons unbleached all-purpose flour

¼ teaspoon kosher salt

CORNMEAL THYME BISCUITS

¾ cup / 90 g unbleached all-purpose flour

½ cup / 60 g whole wheat flour

½ cup / 65 g fine-ground yellow cornmeal

3 tablespoons natural cane sugar

1½ teaspoons baking powder

¾ teaspoon kosher salt

2 tablespoons chopped fresh thyme

5 tablespoons / 70 g cold unsalted butter, cut into ¼-inch cubes, plus more for greasing the skillet

½ cup / 120 ml plain yogurt, home-made (page 25) or store-bought

½ cup / 120 ml buttermilk

⤙ Preheat the oven to 375°F. Lightly butter a 10-inch cast-iron skillet. Cut each peach half into five slices. In a bowl, toss together the peaches, sugar, lemon juice, and lemon zest and let sit until the sugar has begun to dissolve into the fruit, about 10 minutes.

continued

◦ To make the filling: Add the flour and salt to the peaches and stir to combine. Set aside while preparing the dough.

◦ To make the biscuits: In a bowl, sift together the flours, cornmeal, sugar, baking powder, and salt. Add the butter and incorporate it, using your fingertips, until the mixture is the consistency of coarse meal (it's okay if it contains some pea-sized bits, too). Add the yogurt and buttermilk and stir until the dough just comes together.

◦ To assemble and bake the cobbler: Pour the peaches into the prepared pan. Drop small mounds of dough, about 3 tablespoons each, onto the fruit. This yields 7 to 8 biscuits, so someone at the breakfast table will get to sneak an extra on top of their peaches.

◦ Bake until the biscuits are golden brown on top and the peach juice is thickening and bubbling, 30 to 40 minutes. Remove from the oven and let cool for at least 20 minutes before serving.

◦ Serve warm or at room temperature. This cobbler is really best enjoyed the day it's made. The texture of the biscuits changes after a day or so on the counter.

WHAT TO DO WITH LEFTOVER BUTTERMILK?

I always disliked recipes that call for a small amount of buttermilk because I'd be left with a container that would often go bad. Today, I consider it a good reason to make Whole-Grain Buttermilk Pancakes (page 36) or Huckleberry Cornmeal Custard (page 124). Alternatively, you can always freeze leftover buttermilk until you're ready to use it again (thaw it overnight in the refrigerator).

Blueberry Breakfast Bars

These are the ultimate all-purpose breakfast bars. They blend right in with a weekend brunch spread but are also the perfect help-get-me-through-morning-traffic snack. They boast a toasty flavor from the almonds and sesame seeds and a warm fragrance from the marriage of brown sugar and oats. While I love using fresh berries in the summer, in the dead of winter I rely on frozen blueberries I've stored from previous farmers' market hauls.

MAKES 12 TO 16 BARS, DEPENDING ON SIZE

Morning Notes: If you can't find rye flakes, feel free to use more rolled oats instead.

BLUEBERRY FILLING

3 cups / 720 ml fresh blueberries or
    1 (12-ounce / 350 g) package frozen
    blueberries, unthawed

¼ cup / 45 g natural cane sugar

3 tablespoons unbleached
    all-purpose flour

2 tablespoons freshly squeezed
    lemon juice

1 tablespoon grated lemon zest

1 teaspoon water

WHOLE-GRAIN CRUST

½ cup / 50 g rolled oats

1 cup / 100 g rye flakes

¾ cup / 60 g sliced raw almonds

¼ cup / 30 g raw sesame seeds

1 cup / 120 g whole wheat flour

½ cup / 75 g packed light brown sugar

½ teaspoon ground cinnamon

1 teaspoon kosher salt

¾ teaspoon baking powder

1 large egg, beaten

8 tablespoons / 115 g cold unsalted
    butter, cut into ¼-inch cubes,
    plus more for greasing the pan

3 to 4 tablespoons ice water

❧ Preheat the oven to 350°F. Butter an 8-inch square pan.

❧ To prepare the filling: In a heavy-bottomed saucepan, combine the berries, sugar, flour, lemon juice, lemon zest, and water. Stir over medium heat until the mixture begins to simmer. Continue stirring until berries just begin to break down and the sauce thickens, 3 to 4 minutes. Remove from the heat.

❧ To prepare the crust: In the bowl of a food processor fitted with the metal blade, pulse together the rolled oats, rye flakes, almonds, and sesame seeds just until they form a chunky, mealy texture, about 30 seconds. Add the flour, brown sugar, cinnamon, salt, and baking powder and pulse a time or two to combine. Add the egg and butter and pulse until the mixture has the consistency of large crumbs.

continued

⟩ To assemble and bake the bars: Press approximately half of the crust mixture evenly into the bottom of the prepared baking pan. Pour the berry filling onto the crust and spread evenly. Scatter the remaining crust mixture across the top as you would for a fruit crisp or crumble—messy and haphazard, but evenly dispersed. Don't worry about pressing down; it will bake into the bars beautifully.

⟩ Bake until the top crumble is golden brown, about 30 minutes. Let cool completely in the pan. Slice into bars. If wrapped and kept at room temperature, the bars will keep for 3 days.

Make It Your Own: *Try these with your favorite seasonal berries. Blackberries or huckleberries would be lovely, as would cherries.*

Apricot Cherry Compote

Although by definition this is a compote, I think of it much more as a spoonable fruity mess of summer kissed by lemon and dotted with fragrant, toasty almonds. I love cooking cherries with a little balsamic vinegar because it draws out their natural sweetness and gives them a slightly tart kick. Try spooning this on your bowl of yogurt, oatmeal, or muesli. It's also wonderful spread on a slice of toasted seedy bread for a quick on-the-go breakfast. MAKES ABOUT 2 CUPS

1 pound / 450 g apricots
   (7 to 8 medium), pitted and
   quartered (about 2¼ cups / 540 ml)

1 pound / 450 g fresh cherries,
   stemmed and pitted (about 2½ cups /
   600 ml)

⅓ cup / 60 g natural cane sugar

1 teaspoon balsamic vinegar

1 tablespoon water

1 tablespoon freshly squeezed
   lemon juice

1 tablespoon grated lemon zest

Pinch of kosher salt

Pinch of ground cinnamon

½ cup / 70 g blanched slivered
   almonds, toasted (see page 12)

Put the apricots, cherries, sugar, vinegar, water, lemon juice, lemon zest, salt, and cinnamon in a heavy-bottomed saucepan. Over medium heat, bring to a simmer, stirring occasionally. Cover, decrease the heat to low, and simmer until the compote has thickened and most of the liquid has evaporated, 20 to 25 minutes. Stir occasionally to avoid sticking.

Stir in the almonds. Remove from the heat and let stand uncovered for at least 1 hour—plenty of time for the juices to fully thicken. Serve warm or at room temperature. Store in an airtight container in the refrigerator for up to 3 weeks, or in the freezer for up to 6 months.

Roasted Black Cherries

During the months of July and August, if you head east of Seattle on Route 2 for about an hour, you'll come across a handful of little roadside cherry stands with local Rainier and black Bing cherries for one dollar a basket. After a long hike, we usually pick up a few baskets, snacking on them during the ride home and saving enough for breakfast the next morning. If you've never roasted cherries, it draws out their natural flavors and makes them juicy and soft—the little jewels you'll take from the oven will turn even the most humble bowl of porridge or yogurt into a summer occasion. MAKES 1½ CUPS

1 pound / 450 g pitted fresh or
    unthawed frozen black cherries
    (about 2½ cups / 600 ml)

1 tablespoon freshly squeezed
    lemon juice

3 tablespoons honey

Generous pinch of kosher salt

Freshly ground black pepper (optional)

⇢ Preheat the oven to 375°F.

⇢ In a large bowl, combine the cherries, lemon juice, honey, salt, and a few grinds of pepper and mix well. Turn out onto a glass pie plate or baking dish so the berries nestle together and cook in their juices.

⇢ Bake until the cherries have softened and the juices are beginning to thicken, about 15 minutes. Stir every 5 minutes or so to prevent sticking. Serve warm or at room temperature, or let cool and refrigerate in an airtight container for up to 3 days.

Stewed Red Currants

I could never find currants in the Bay Area, so it was quite a treat to come across them in Seattle. Because they have such a brief season, snatch them up in late summer and gather a crew of small hands to help you remove them from their stalks. When stewed, currants are extra juicy—almost syrupy, really—and wonderfully tart. Use them in place of your favorite jam. MAKES ABOUT 1 CUP

2½ cups / 275 g red currants

3 tablespoons natural cane sugar

1 tablespoon water

1 teaspoon freshly squeezed lemon juice

Rinse the currants well and remove them from their stalks. Put them in a small heavy-bottomed saucepan and add the sugar, water, and lemon juice. Bring to a simmer over medium heat, stirring occasionally to make sure the currants don't stick to the pan. Once the mixture has begun to bubble ever so slightly, decrease the heat to low and let cook until the currants have started to release their juices and pop, 5 to 6 minutes. The mixture will look a little juicier than you might think it should. Don't worry; it's not supposed to be thick like jam, and it will come together a bit as it cools. Let cool and refrigerate for up to 1 week.

Blueberry Sauce

During the summer I always keep a jar of this blueberry sauce in the refrigerator. It's juicier and looser than jam and not too sweet, with a hint of citrus. The secret to this sauce is letting your berries simmer slowly for at least eight minutes. As they do, their juices thicken and they settle into one another. Once cool, this sauce is good spooned onto just about everything: yogurt, porridge, pancakes, waffles, and crepes. Make a double batch—trust me on this. MAKES ABOUT 2 CUPS

1 pound / 450 g fresh or frozen
    blueberries (about 3 cups / 720 ml)
1 tablespoon grated orange zest

1 tablespoon honey
⅓ cup / 60 g natural cane sugar

⤳ Combine all the ingredients in a small saucepan. Cook over medium heat until the mixture begins to slowly bubble and boil. Decrease the heat to low and simmer until the mixture begins to thicken, about 8 minutes. Remove from the heat. Serve warm or room temperature, or let cool and store in an airtight container in the refrigerator for up to 3 weeks, or in the freezer for up to 6 months.

FALL
gathering

BUSY WEEKDAYS

Nutty Millet Breakfast Cookies 106

Warm Farro Breakfast Bowl with Apples,
Cranberries, and Hazelnuts 109

Hasty Pudding with Golden Raisins and Pepitas 110

Peanut Butter Crispy Brown Rice Bars 113

SLOW SUNDAYS

Creamy Breakfast Rice with Honey-Poached Figs
and Pistachios 114

Red Flannel Buckwheat Hash 116

Buckwheat Crepes with Honeyed Ricotta
and Sautéed Plums 118

BRUNCH

Baked Pumpkin Risotto 121

Huckleberry Cornmeal Custard 124

Bulgur-Stuffed Baked Apples with
Walnuts and Raisins 126

Fresh Fig Parfaits with Popped Amaranth
and Almond Cream 128

SPREADS AND TOPPINGS

Honeyed Ricotta 131

Dark Chocolate Hazelnut Spread 133

Spiced Pear Sauce 134

WHEN I WAS YOUNG, on the first Sunday that felt like fall my family would load into the station wagon and my dad would drive out to Mr. Wrigley's apple farm. My sisters and I would clamor out of the car and race up to the booth. There, Mr. Wrigley would eye each kid in line up and down and, based on his instant assessment of what kind of apple eater you might be, he'd hand select the perfect variety for you. We'd take bags home to snack on, and my mom would busy herself making applesauce, apple cake, and apple butter.

After some fifty years presiding over the apples, Mr. Wrigley passed on, leaving the orchards to a bushel of younger Wrigleys. Today, because I live a few states away, I have a different gauge of the changing season. I always know fall has arrived not with a trip to the apple orchard, but with the crisp nights and unexpected—often impromptu— gathering of a few friends in the kitchen. Maybe over dark beers, bread, and cheese. Sometimes over a real meal and good wine.

The kitchen is simply where so many of us are comfortable. However warm or sterile, crowded or solitary, stocked or empty—it's a room that naturally draws people together. I think of fall in much the same way: regardless of where I am—in Boston for graduate school or San Francisco for work—it's a season of coming back indoors, break- ing out board games at night, and starting to notice the light changing ever so slowly, but surely.

When I lived in Oakland, my kitchen was barely large enough to do a halfhearted pirouette, but without fail, it was where people gathered. One crisp fall night when Sam was visiting, we decided to host a soup party. We made two big pots of soup and I braved the rain to run out and buy a few baguettes and butter. My friend Holly made a large caramel cake, I baked fudgy brownies, and other friends brought wine and good cheese. After everyone arrived, the apartment windows began steaming up, sweaters came off, and sure enough—everyone was crowded into the tiny kitchen clutching bowls of soup. On nights like that, the meal doesn't even really matter. It's the company. It's the gathering.

SEASONAL *Spotlight*

Indian summers are common in both the Bay Area and Seattle, so early fall is often sunny and warm. Although they make a quick early showing in the summer, I associate **figs** with the fall. They don't ripen well off the tree, so select ripe figs, refrigerate them, and try to use them quickly. When perfectly ripe, figs should feel plump and tender but shouldn't be sticky on the outside. **Plums** are wonderful for fall baking and snacking. If you can find Italian or prune plums, they hold their shape well when cooked and have a beautiful dark purple color.

Later in the season, I look forward to classic fall fruits like **pears** and **apples**. While I usually bake with Granny Smith or Honeycrisp apples, I keep an eye out for heirloom and local varieties like Lodi, Winesap, Newtown, Pippin, and Northern Spy for snacking. As for pears, Bartlett and Anjou are great for baking.

Huckleberries, those little jewels that look like mini blueberries but taste sweeter and more complex, are always worth the splurge. Swirl them into yogurt, fold them into muffin batter, or scatter them over ice cream. **Pomegranates** add a messy but welcome pop of color to morning fruit salads. Refrigerate them whole for up to one month, the seeds for up to a few days. **Pumpkins** are used for everything from roasting to baking, making their way into quick breads, pies, and colorful side dishes. Just be sure to choose pumpkin varieties that are meant for baking or cooking (these include sugar pumpkins, aka pie pumpkins, and cheese pumpkins, aka Cinderella pumpkins).

Nutty Millet Breakfast Cookies

You know you've done something right when you bake a breakfast cookie that could easily graduate to an afternoon or late-night treat. One that friends and family start requesting for get-togethers and potlucks. A cookie you become known for at your neighborhood coffee shop after dropping a few off for the staff one morning in March. Thomas, one of my favorite baristas and greatest cookie cheerleaders, often subtly legislates for another batch, praising their toasty combination of pecans, walnuts, and raisins. On occasion, I give in. If you haven't worked with millet before, it's packed with fiber, low in fat, naturally gluten-free, and bakes beautifully into this crumbly, soft cookie. Double the recipe and freeze a few to pull out whenever your morning is more bustle than bliss—or to bring to your own neighborhood barista. MAKES 12 TO 14 COOKIES

Morning Notes: *I like using a little barley flour in this recipe because of its almost sweet flavor and light texture, but feel free to substitute additional white whole wheat flour if you prefer.*

1 cup / 120 g white whole wheat flour

¼ cup / 30 g barley flour

¾ cup / 75 g rolled oats

¼ cup / 45 g millet

¼ cup / 15 g wheat bran

½ teaspoon baking soda

½ teaspoon baking powder

1 teaspoon ground cinnamon

¼ teaspoon ground nutmeg

¼ teaspoon ground ginger

½ teaspoon kosher salt

½ cup / 120 ml coconut oil, melted

½ cup / 120 ml maple syrup

1 large egg, beaten

1 teaspoon pure vanilla extract

⅓ cup / 45 g raisins

¼ cup / 25 g walnuts, toasted (see page 12) and coarsely chopped

⅓ cup / 35 g pecans, toasted (see page 12) and coarsely chopped

⤏ Preheat the oven to 350°F. Line a large baking sheet with parchment paper or a silicone mat.

⤏ In a large bowl, whisk together the flours, oats, millet, bran, baking soda, baking powder, cinnamon, nutmeg, ginger, and salt.

⤏ In another bowl, whisk together the melted coconut oil, maple syrup, egg, and vanilla. Add to the flour mixture, folding in with a wooden spoon until incorporated. Stir the raisins, walnuts, and pecans into the dough until evenly dispersed. At this point, I'll often use my hands and almost massage the dough quickly to make sure all of the wet and dry ingredients are combined. Let the dough rest for 10 minutes.

continued

❧ Scoop out between 2 and 3 tablespoons of dough and, working quickly, form a ball with the palms of your hand. (The smaller the cookies, the better they hold their shape.) Place the balls about 1½ inches apart on the prepared baking sheet. Gently flatten the cookies with the palm of your hand to about ¾ inch thick.

❧ Bake until golden brown around the edges and firmed yet still slightly soft in the center (they'll continue to firm up as they cool), about 12 minutes. Let the cookies cool for 10 minutes on the baking sheet, then transfer to a wire rack to cool completely. If kept in an airtight container, they will remain fresh for 3 to 4 days.

Make It Your Own: *Use the base recipe as a vehicle to add your favorite nuts and fruits; pistachios and dried apricots would be wonderful, as would dried cherries and almonds.*

Warm Farro Breakfast Bowl *with* Apples, Cranberries, *and* Hazelnuts

I originally developed this recipe for the website the Kitchn, and it remains the dish that generates the most frequent thank-you emails from readers. The combination of chewy grains, creamy yogurt, tart cranberries, crisp apples, and toasty hazelnuts makes for a special fall breakfast, and one that I return to often during those brisk yet bright mornings in October and November when a warm breakfast becomes requisite. SERVES 2

Morning Notes: *For this recipe, use whichever variety of apple you love. I usually gravitate toward a firm Honeycrisp or Pink Lady. No need to peel them—this is a recipe that's best kept simple and rustic.*

2 tablespoons coconut oil

1 large apple, cored and diced into ½-inch cubes (about 1½ cups / 160 g)

¼ teaspoon ground cinnamon

1 cup / 170 g cooked farro (see page 23)

¼ cup / 30 g hazelnuts, toasted and skinned (see page 12) and chopped

¼ cup / 30 g dried cranberries

¼ cup / 60 ml Greek yogurt, for serving

¼ cup / 60 ml honey, for serving

⇥ In a small saucepan over medium-high heat, warm the coconut oil until it melts. Add the apple and sauté until soft and slightly golden, 5 to 7 minutes. Add the cinnamon and stir to combine. Add the farro, hazelnuts, and cranberries and toss together with the apples until they're coated with the oil and warmed all the way through.

⇥ To serve, scoop a heaping portion of the farro mixture into each bowl and top with a few spoonfuls of the yogurt and a generous drizzle of the honey.

Make It Your Own: *Use any toasted, chopped nuts you like (pistachios or almonds would be wonderful) or experiment with different fresh fruits, like pears or figs, or dried fruits, like currants, dates, or raisins. If you want to experiment with different grains besides farro, try wheat berries, spelt berries, rye berries, or barley (any hearty grain, really).*

Hasty Pudding *with* Golden Raisins *and* Pepitas

Hasty pudding, a simple cornmeal dessert porridge, originated in Britain but was quickly adopted by Colonial Americans for its ease and economy. It resembles a thick porridge and is traditionally served with a little maple syrup or molasses. Its fancier cousin, Indian pudding, is similar, although it calls for raisins, nuts, and warm spices and bakes in the oven for hours. My version straddles these traditions—with a modern twist. It's a warmly spiced cornmeal porridge cooked on the stovetop, with the addition of creamy Greek yogurt and a double wallop of ginger (dried and crystallized) to achieve a velvety texture with a subtle spicy-sweet kick. SERVES 4 TO 6

Morning Notes: *Use a taller pot than you think you need here—the pudding will spatter a bit.*

1½ cups / 360 ml milk

2½ cups / 600 ml water,
  plus more if necessary

1 cup / 165 g polenta or stone-ground
  coarse cornmeal

½ teaspoon kosher salt

¼ teaspoon ground ginger

¼ teaspoon ground cinnamon

¾ cup / 105 g golden raisins

3 tablespoons chopped
  crystallized ginger

½ cup / 120 ml Greek yogurt

¼ cup / 35 g pepitas, toasted
  (see page 12)

2 to 3 tablespoons honey, for serving
  (optional)

1 to 2 tablespoons unsalted butter,
  for serving (optional)

⤙ In a large heavy-bottomed saucepan over medium heat, bring the milk and water to a gentle boil. Add the polenta, salt, ground ginger, and cinnamon and whisk to combine. Decrease the heat to medium-low. Simmer until the pudding is thick and creamy, 25 to 30 minutes, stirring often to prevent sticking or clumping. Add more water, 2 tablespoons at a time, if the mixture starts clumping or sticking to the bottom of the pan or seems too thick. You're ultimately going for a texture that's creamy and stir-able—a little looser than mashed potatoes but thick enough to perch upright on your spoon.

⤙ When the pudding is almost done, stir in the golden raisins so they have a chance to soften slightly. Fold in the crystallized ginger and yogurt. Scoop into individual serving bowls and top with the pepitas. Add a drizzle of the honey and a dab of the butter if desired.

Make Ahead: *I find polenta and cornmeal puddings are really best eaten on the day they're made, but you can certainly keep this in an airtight container in the refrigerator for a few days. To reheat, you'll need additional liquid. Start with 1 to 2 tablespoons of water on the stovetop and stir vigorously. Add more liquid if necessary. I don't suggest reheating in the microwave.*

GRITS OR POLENTA:
What's the Difference?

Both polenta and grits are made from stone-ground cornmeal: dried corn that's ground down into smaller, coarse bits. So how do the two differ? Some people think the difference lies in geography: the Italian version is known as polenta, whereas the Southern version is known as grits. Others think that polenta is made with yellow corn, while grits are always made with white corn. Generally speaking, the grind of the corn is a big distinguishing factor when discussing the difference between polenta and grits. When coarsely ground, they are packaged as grits; when ground finer, they're packaged as polenta.

The folks at Anson Mills, my favorite brand for stone-ground cornmeal, go into more detail. They use different types of corn for different products. Most grits in the South are traditionally made from a class of corn called **dent corn** (which is a bit softer and therefore mills more easily), whereas in Italy, most polenta is made from a class of corn called **flint corn**, which holds its texture better. The result of these different classes? Grits are traditionally creamier and mushier, depending on who is making them, of course. And polenta has a more toothsome quality.

For the recipes in this book, you can't go wrong with a coarse-ground cornmeal, but you do want to make sure it's labeled "whole-grain." Check out your local bulk bins, Bob's Red Mill, or Anson Mills for more of a splurge (see Sources, page 166).

A Good Place to Start
- Hasty Pudding with Golden Raisins and Pepitas (page 110)
- Bacon and Kale Polenta Squares (page 65)
- Huckleberry Cornmeal Custard (page 124)
- Smoked Salmon Crème Fraîche Tart with a Cornmeal Millet Crust (page 63)

Peanut Butter Crispy Brown Rice Bars

Crisped brown rice, peanut butter, and honey replace puffed white rice and marshmallows in these quick, no-bake bars. A hit with kids and adults alike, they boast toasted sesame seeds and roasted peanuts for added crunch—simultaneously satisfying those sweet and salty cravings. The nice thing about these bars is they can be a great clean-out-the-pantry recipe. I'm always tossing in a few leftover nuts or dried fruits I have on hand, and may have even been known to stir in dark chocolate chips on occasion for more afternoon-appropriate snacking. Because they're not bound by gooey marshmallows, these bars are a bit softer than more traditional crisped rice bars and require about an hour in the fridge for easier slicing. MAKES 12 TO 15 BARS, DEPENDING ON SIZE

Morning Notes: *Look for unsweetened crispy brown rice cereal. And while I like using natural peanut butters, for this recipe I use a brand that doesn't require stirring in the oil. Justin's brand is great because it's super creamy yet not oily, and doesn't contain additional salt or sugar.*

2 tablespoons butter, plus more for greasing the pan

¾ cup / 180 ml honey

¾ cup / 180 ml brown rice syrup

1½ cups / 360 ml unsweetened peanut butter

½ cup / 60 g sesame seeds, toasted (see page 12)

6 cups / 100 g cups crispy brown rice cereal

1 cup / 140 g chopped dry-roasted peanuts

1 teaspoon kosher salt

❧ Butter a 9 by 13-inch baking dish and set aside. In a saucepan, combine the butter, honey, brown rice syrup, and peanut butter. Cook over medium heat, stirring occasionally, until warmed and combined.

❧ In a very large bowl, combine the sesame seeds, cereal, peanuts, and salt. Pour the peanut butter mixture over the dry ingredients and stir until combined. Spoon the mixture into the prepared pan and, using the back of a spatula, press to create a nice, even layer. Refrigerate for at least 1 hour before cutting into bars in the pan. Cover and store at room temperature for 3 to 4 days.

Creamy Breakfast Rice *with* Honey-Poached Figs *and* Pistachios

Rice pudding is one of my ultimate comfort foods, so developing this creamy whole-grain breakfast rice was a real treat, and I now turn to this recipe year-round. It's not too sweet on its own, relying instead on the earthy flavor of ripe fall figs. While many people prepare breakfast rice by actually cooking the rice in milk, I love this cheater's version because it uses cooked rice that's quickly heated in a pot of milk, so it gets super creamy and soft while still maintaining its characteristic chew. I'll often make a double batch of rice for dinner in the evening, knowing I want to get a pot of this going the next morning.

SERVES 4

Morning Notes: *Poaching figs is simple, but there's a fine line between perfectly poached and overdone. I poach figs with the stems on and remove them later—this will help keep them from getting mushy. Smaller figs cook quicker. Ultimately, you want the figs soft but not splitting or bursting open—always a delicate balance. Erring on the side of underpoaching is preferable.*

FIGS

3 cups water

¾ cup / 180 ml honey

½ teaspoon kosher salt

10 washed ripe fresh figs
(about 8.5 ounces / 240 g;
I like black Mission or Brown Turkey)

CREAMY RICE

3 cups / 400 g cooked long-grain brown rice (see page 23)

1½ cups / 360 ml whole milk or nut milk (low-fat or nonfat milk will make a thinner rice)

2 tablespoons maple syrup

1 teaspoon pure vanilla extract

¼ teaspoon ground cinnamon

¼ teaspoon kosher salt

⅓ cup / 45 g pistachios, chopped

❧ To poach the figs: Bring the water, honey, and salt to a boil over medium-high heat in a small saucepan. Decrease the heat to medium-low and simmer, stirring occasionally, until the liquid begins to reduce and thicken to the consistency of a light syrup, about 20 minutes. Ultimately, you should be left with about 1¾ cups liquid. Set the figs into the honey syrup. To poach the figs successfully, you want to make sure they're mostly covered in liquid, so if you need to switch to a smaller saucepan, now is the time. Simmer over medium-low heat until tender, 8 to 10 minutes, gently turning them and scooting them around so each side is poached evenly. Using a slotted spoon, transfer the figs to a plate to cool slightly. Once cool enough to touch, carefully slice off the stems and cut the figs in half.

❧ To make the rice: In a heavy-bottomed saucepan over medium heat, combine the cooked rice, milk, maple syrup, vanilla, cinnamon, and salt and cook, uncovered, until the mixture begins to thicken, 10 to 12 minutes. Stir occasionally to avoid sticking. Note that this should be a looser, almost milky dish: the rice won't soak up all of the liquid, and it will continue to thicken off the heat. Remove from the heat and let sit for a few minutes to cool ever so slightly and firm up a bit.

❧ To serve: Divide the rice between 4 bowls. Top with the poached figs and the pistachios. I like to spoon a bit of the syrupy poaching liquid over the top of each bowl, too. If you have leftover rice, reheat it the next morning, adding a dash more milk.

Red Flannel Buckwheat Hash

There's a bustling corner breakfast café in San Francisco's Dogpatch neighborhood that serves strong coffee, fluffy buckwheat pancakes, and a show-stopping red flannel hash. Traditionally, this New England breakfast is made with corned beef or brisket, potatoes, and beets. My version replaces the brisket and white potatoes with a little bacon and sweet potatoes. After the potatoes and beets crisp up, I stir in earthy buckwheat groats at the very end and top it all with fresh herbs and a soft-fried egg. It's a hearty breakfast, so it's usually reserved for slow weekends. Leftovers? Even better the next day. SERVES 4

Morning Notes: *The cooking times for this hash are more of a guide than a hard-and-fast rule. The longer you cook it, the softer and more crumbly it becomes—just watch that the temperature isn't too high so it doesn't burn.*

2 medium sweet potatoes, peeled, rinsed, and diced into ½-inch cubes (5 cups / 700 g)

3 small red beets, peeled and diced into ¼-inch cubes (1¾ cups / 240 g)

2 tablespoons chopped fresh dill, plus more for serving

1 teaspoon kosher salt

Freshly ground black pepper

5 ounces / 140 g thick-cut bacon, chopped

1 cup / 120 g chopped yellow onion (about ½ large onion)

2 cloves garlic, minced

1 cup / 170 g cooked buckwheat groats (see page 22)

¼ cup / 60 ml crème fraîche, for serving (optional)

2 tablespoons chopped fresh chives, for serving

4 fried eggs (optional; see page 86)

❧ In a large bowl, stir together the sweet potatoes, beets, dill, and salt. Season with pepper. Set aside.

❧ In a large nonstick pan over medium heat, cook the bacon until brown and crisp, 5 to 7 minutes. Using a slotted spoon, transfer the bacon to a plate lined with paper towels. Drain the bacon drippings from the skillet, reserving just enough to coat the bottom of the pan (about 2 tablespoons).

❧ In the same skillet, sauté the onion over medium heat until just soft and translucent, 3 to 4 minutes. Add the garlic and cook for another minute. Pour the sweet potato mixture into the skillet and stir so it combines with the cooked onion. Scoot it around so it forms a nice even layer in the skillet. Use a spatula to press down the layer so it's flat and snug.

Cover the pan and cook until the beets and sweet potatoes are fork-tender, 25 to 30 minutes, flipping the hash after about 15 minutes so both sides brown evenly. After flipping as best you can, press the potatoes and beets down into the skillet again. Don't worry if the potatoes or beets start to fall apart a bit—it's a rustic dish, and that will likely happen.

ᴥ Once the beets and potatoes are fork-tender, stir in the cooked bacon and buckwheat. Taste and season with more salt and pepper if desired.

ᴥ To serve, scoop into 4 individual bowls, dollop with crème fraîche, and sprinkle with the chives and additional dill. I'll often top mine with a soft-fried egg.

Make It Your Own: *You really can't go wrong in making this hash exactly how you want it. Love white potatoes? Use them instead. Green onions and leeks are lovely, cubed zucchini adds a splash of color, and spinach or kale softens into this hash right before serving for an even heartier meal. You can easily make it vegetarian by omitting the bacon and cooking the onion in 2 tablespoons of olive oil instead of bacon drippings.*

Buckwheat Crepes *with* Honeyed Ricotta *and* Sautéed Plums

My friend Keena lives less than a mile away and has a plum tree she can't keep up with. In early fall, she makes jam with as many plums as she can and sends me home with a big grocery bag full of them every time I see her. I'm not much of a canner, so I began sautéing them and using them as a topping for yogurt and porridge, and as a filling for these simple buckwheat crepes. While buckwheat groats have a pretty distinct flavor and can be a hard sell for many folks, buckwheat flour is commonly used and adored in both sweet and savory crepes. For this recipe, use oval-shaped Italian plums (or prune plums) if you can; they're nice and firm and lend themselves well to sautéing—or just plain snacking.

MAKES ABOUT 12 CREPES

> **Morning Notes:** *The crepe batter needs to rest for at least an hour, so plan accordingly or make the batter and refrigerate it overnight. If you go that route, the crepes cook best when the batter is at room temperature, so let it sit out for at least 30 minutes before cooking them.*

CREPES

¹⁄₂ cup / 65 g buckwheat flour

¹⁄₂ cup / 60 g unbleached all-purpose flour

¹⁄₂ teaspoon kosher salt

1 cup / 240 ml milk

³⁄₄ cup / 180 ml buttermilk

2 tablespoons butter, melted, plus more for greasing the pan

2 large eggs

1 tablespoons coconut oil or butter

SAUTÉED PLUMS

¹⁄₂ teaspoon pure vanilla extract

1 tablespoon honey

1 pound / 450 g Italian plums (6 to 7 plums), each sliced into 6 wedges

Honeyed Ricotta (page 131)

Honey, for serving

❧ To make the crepes: Whisk the flours, salt, milk, buttermilk, butter, and eggs together in a large bowl until very smooth. To save arm power, you can blend the ingredients in a blender instead. Let the batter sit for at least 1 hour at room temperature and up to 1 day in the refrigerator.

❧ Rub a small dab of butter (¹⁄₂ tablespoon or so) onto the bottom of a 9- or 10-inch nonstick crepe pan or sauté pan over medium heat and wait until it melts completely. (Too much butter will make for a soggy crepe.) Pour ¹⁄₄ cup of the batter into the hot pan and tilt

continued

it in a circular motion to ensure the batter spreads out into an even layer. Cook over low heat until the edges start to pull away from the pan, about 2 minutes. Using a nonstick spatula, carefully flip and cook the other side until golden brown, about 1 minute. Lay the crepe on a large plate and repeat until you've gone through all of the batter (it's okay to stack the crepes on the plate). If the crepe pan starts to get too dry, add another little dab of butter. I tend to cook these quickly while the plums are sautéing and assemble them right then, but if you're chatting with friends and taking your time, keep the finished, unfilled crepes warm in a 200°F oven until ready to assemble.

❧ To sauté the plums: In a medium saucepan over medium heat, melt the coconut oil. Add the vanilla and honey, swirl the pan so they combine with the coconut oil, and then add the plums. Sauté until juicy and warm, 2 to 3 minutes.

❧ To assemble: For each crepe, gently fold the crepe in fourths (fold in half, then in half again) and dollop 1 to 2 tablespoons of the Honeyed Ricotta and a few sautéed plums on top. Finish with a generous drizzle of honey.

Make It Your Own: *These crepes work in any season. Swap out the plums for stone fruit in the summer or pears and cranberries in the winter. For a more decadent brunch, I've used mascarpone thinned with just a little Greek yogurt as a topping instead of the ricotta. Alternatively, try a spoonful of Dark Chocolate Hazelnut Spread (page 133) or, for a jammy filling, try Apricot Cherry Compote (page 98) or Strawberry Rhubarb Quick Jam (page 71). For a savory option, make wraps filled with the Greens and Grains Scramble (page 140).*

Make Ahead: *You can cook the crepes and store them in the refrigerator, stacked between pieces of waxed or parchment paper, for up to 3 days. You can also freeze them for up to 3 months by allowing the crepes to cool completely, wrapping them well in plastic wrap, and placing them in an airtight container. To reheat, place them in a glass baking dish or a pie plate covered with aluminum foil. Heat in a 250°F oven until just warmed through.*

Baked Pumpkin Risotto

Usually risotto is cooked on the stovetop, requiring a great deal of stirring to reach the perfect consistency. This version is a very different affair. It's baked in the oven and requires virtually no tending yet still has the soft, creamy texture of a traditional risotto. While it adds a bit of time to the overall preparation, I let the onion caramelize so it develops that characteristic deep, smoky sweetness that makes it well worth the wait. The sweetness of apple juice in the cooking liquid beautifully balances the tart sour cream. The result is a fall-spiced brunch dish that you can put in the oven and virtually forget about. SERVES 8

Morning Notes: *Arborio rice is traditional for risotto, but it's not technically a whole grain. Here, I've opted for a short-grain brown rice, which still has the bran and germ intact, so you're getting the best of both worlds—a surprisingly creamy risotto and whole grain nutrition. I parboil the rice to soften and plump up the kernels so they fully soak up all the cooking liquid. Do this while you caramelize the onion, and you're looking at about 30 minutes of hands-on cooking time: my kind of brunch recipe.*

1 tablespoon unsalted butter, plus more for greasing the baking dish

1 tablespoon extra-virgin olive oil

1 cup / 120 g peeled and thinly sliced yellow onion (about ½ large onion)

2 cups / 420 g short-grain brown rice (sweet brown rice also works well)

1 (15-ounce / 425 g) can pumpkin puree (not pumpkin pie filling), about 1¾ cups / 420 ml

¼ cup / 60 ml sour cream

1 tablespoon maple syrup

¼ teaspoon ground ginger

½ teaspoon ground cinnamon

½ teaspoon ground nutmeg

2 teaspoons kosher salt

Pinch of freshly ground black pepper

2¾ cups / 660 ml apple juice

3 cups / 720 ml water

¼ cup / 15 g shredded Parmesan cheese, for serving (optional)

¾ cup / 90 g hazelnuts, toasted and skinned (see page 12) and chopped, for serving (optional)

⇥ Preheat the oven to 375°F. Butter a 9 by 13-inch baking dish.

⇥ To caramelize the onion: Warm the butter and olive oil in a large skillet over medium heat until they've melted into one another. Add the onion, stirring to coat in the oil and butter. Decrease the heat to low and let the onion cook until dark golden brown, about 25 minutes. You want to stir as little as possible, but certainly stir enough to avoid burning or sticking to the bottom of the pan.

continued

⊰ Meanwhile, to parboil the rice, bring a pot of salted water to a boil over high heat. Stir in the rice, decrease the heat to medium (the water should remain at a nice, low boil), and cook until the rice is half tender and enlarged, 12 to 15 minutes. Drain and set aside.

⊰ To prepare the risotto: In a large bowl, whisk together the pumpkin, sour cream, maple syrup, ginger, cinnamon, nutmeg, salt, and pepper until creamy. Fold in the caramelized onion and parboiled rice. Scoop the mixture into the prepared baking dish and smooth it out in a nice, even layer.

⊰ In a saucepan, heat the apple juice and water together over medium-high heat until barely boiling. Pour the mixture over the top of the rice. Do not stir. Transfer the pan to the oven. It will be pretty full, so be careful when placing it in the oven. Alternatively, place the pan inside the oven, then slowly pour in the liquid.

⊰ Bake, uncovered, for about 40 minutes. The risotto will likely be a touch loose and still have a layer of liquid on top when you pull it from the oven—this is perfect. It will continue to soak up the liquid as it cools.

⊰ Let cool for 15 minutes before serving. Taste and adjust the seasoning if necessary. Serve warm. Sprinkle generously with the Parmesan and hazelnuts. While I do think this dish is best enjoyed the day it's made (and right after cooling briefly, if possible), you can cover and refrigerate leftovers for up to 3 days.

Huckleberry Cornmeal Custard

Sam used to work at a Seattle restaurant called Boat Street, where they made a wonderful cornmeal custard—a simple mixture of milk, cream, cornmeal, and eggs. Our friend Molly Wizenberg wrote about a similar recipe in her book *A Homemade Life*, noting its original appearance in Marion Cunningham's *The Breakfast Book*. When we were dating long-distance, Sam would make his tweaked version of the custard for me when I'd come and visit in the cooler months. And now I've altered his version even further by using a touch more cornmeal, a few glugs of buttermilk, and oat flour, which I love for its mild, slightly sweet flavor. So you see how these things go: when something's that good, it gets around.

For a short time in September, you may be able to find huckleberries at farmers' markets. For this dish, they're spread in the bottom of the pan, and while baking, they magically rise to the top and the cream rises to the middle, resulting in a beautifully layered affair—midway between a cake, a custard, and a clafoutis. It's great reheated, so we've been known to make it for just ourselves on a gray Sunday when it seems this is the only breakfast that will do. SERVES 6 TO 8

Morning Notes: *This batter fits perfectly into a 10-inch pie pan with 2-inch sides or a 9-inch cake pan (they have slightly higher walls). Don't be tempted to use a standard shallow 9-inch pie pan; there's simply too much batter.*

3 tablespoons unsalted butter, plus more for greasing the pan	1½ cups / 360 ml whole milk
¾ cup / 75 g oat flour	½ cup / 120 ml buttermilk
1 cup / 160 g medium-ground cornmeal	1½ tablespoons distilled white vinegar
1 teaspoon baking powder	2 teaspoons grated lemon zest
½ teaspoon baking soda	2 teaspoons pure vanilla extract
2 large eggs, beaten	1¼ cups / 300 ml fresh huckleberries or blueberries
¼ cup / 45 g natural cane sugar	¾ cup / 180 ml heavy cream
1 teaspoon kosher salt	Grade B maple syrup, for serving

❧ Preheat the oven to 350°F. Butter a deep-dish 10-inch pie pan. Place the buttered dish in the oven to warm while you make the batter.

❧ In a small dish, melt the 3 tablespoons butter in the microwave on high heat, about 45 seconds. Be careful not to let it splatter. Pour into a large bowl and set aside to cool for a few minutes.

❧ Meanwhile, in a small bowl, whisk together the flour, cornmeal, baking powder, and baking soda. Set aside.

❧ Add the eggs to the butter and whisk to blend well. Add the sugar, salt, milk, buttermilk, vinegar, lemon zest, and vanilla and whisk well. Whisking constantly, add the flour mixture. Mix until the batter is smooth.

❧ Remove the heated pan from the oven and set on a baking sheet for easy transport to and from the oven. Spoon the berries into the bottom of the pan in an even layer. Pour the batter on top of the berries. Then ever so slowly pour the cream into the center of the batter. Don't stir. Carefully slide the pan into the oven, taking care not to jostle it, and bake until golden brown on top, 50 to 60 minutes. Cool for 10 to 15 minutes to allow the custard to set up.

❧ Serve warm with a generous drizzle of maple syrup. Cover and refrigerate leftovers for up to 4 days (but insist on warming them before serving!).

Make It Your Own: *Certainly substitute blueberries if you can't track down huckleberries.*

Bulgur-Stuffed Baked Apples
with Walnuts *and* Raisins

Typically, baked apple recipes are considered a dessert, but this whole-grain version makes for a satisfying breakfast. The warmly spiced bulgur wheat is high in fiber, and the apples are sweetened solely with a touch of maple syrup. Because bulgur wheat is so quick cooking, these are oven ready in about fifteen minutes. While I like these stuffed apples best when they're warm, they're quite tasty at room temperature, too, and are a nice addition to any breakfast party spread. SERVES 4

Morning Notes: *In late September, Honeycrisp apples are usually the first local variety to start popping up at the market in Washington. Crisp, mottled, and not too sweet, they're great for baking, but you can certainly use any firm apple (avoid Golden Delicious, as they're too soft and can fall apart easily in the oven). Do know that the larger your apples, the longer the baking time will be for this recipe.*

1¼ cups / 300 ml apple juice

¼ cup / 40 g bulgur wheat

1 teaspoon grated lemon zest

4 firm apples (such as Honeycrisp
   or Granny Smith)

½ cup / 50 g raw walnut halves,
   coarsely chopped

¼ cup / 35 g raisins

½ teaspoon pure vanilla extract

½ teaspoon ground cinnamon

¼ teaspoon ground ginger

2 tablespoons maple syrup

2 tablespoons honey, for serving
   (optional)

⇥ Preheat the oven to 350°F.

⇥ In a small saucepan, bring ½ cup of the apple juice to a boil over medium-high heat. Add the bulgur and stir well. Cover tightly, remove from the heat, and let sit for 10 minutes to allow the bulgur to soften and absorb most of the liquid (recall that bulgur doesn't require any active cooking time). Drain the bulgur in a fine-mesh sieve to get rid of any extra liquid. Scoop the bulgur into a small bowl and stir in the lemon zest.

⇥ Slice ½ inch off the top of each apple and reserve. Using a melon baller or very sturdy spoon, scoop out the core from each apple, leaving the bottoms intact. After coring the apples, continue to scoop out a well for the filling, but be careful to leave at least ½ inch of flesh around the sides of the apples so they don't collapse while baking, reserving the scooped out apple flesh. Chop ¼ cup of the scooped-out apple flesh and set aside to add to the filling. Discard (or snack on) the rest.

❧ Remove the stems from the reserved apple tops with a paring knife (the stems might have already come off when the tops were sliced off). In a small bowl, stir together the bulgur, walnuts, raisins, vanilla, cinnamon, ginger, and the ¼ cup of chopped apple. Divide the filling evenly among the apples and cover with their tops. Be generous with the filling—it's okay if the apples are heaping. Place them in an 8-inch square baking dish.

❧ In a small saucepan, heat the remaining ¾ cup apple juice and the maple syrup until warm. Pour the mixture over the top of the apples.

❧ Bake for 15 minutes, then baste the apples with their cooking liquid and bake until tender, an additional 5 to 10 minutes.

❧ Serve warm, spooning the pan juices over the top of each apple and drizzling generously with the honey.

Fresh Fig Parfaits *with* Popped Amaranth *and* Almond Cream

This dairy-free breakfast was originally inspired by a Theo chocolate bar made with almonds, figs, and fresh fennel. The Theo factory is located in Seattle, and whenever I pick up cacao nibs for Marge, I sneak in and grab a few samples. In our house, we serve everything from glasses of wine to ice cream in mason jars, so I often grab for the small, 8-ounce jars when making these parfaits. But when having friends over, I'll opt for pretty parfait glasses or good old-fashioned bowls, so use whichever makes you happiest. If raspberries are ripe, they're delicious layered in with the ripe figs, honey-kissed almond cream, toasty almonds, and crunchy popped amaranth. It's worth noting that the almonds for the almond cream take an overnight soak, so plan accordingly. If you're short on time, you can make these with plain yogurt instead of the almond cream. SERVES 4

Morning Notes: *If you've never popped amaranth, it's a simple, quick way to add a little crunch to any morning recipe. The key is to have a very hot, dry pan wide enough so the amaranth can rest in one layer (don't use a low-sided skillet because the grains will jump as they pop). I'll often pop it in two batches, just to make sure each little grain gets prime real estate in the pan. See more details on page 130.*

ALMOND CREAM

1 cup / 140 g raw almonds

¾ cup / 180 ml water, plus more if necessary

1 teaspoon pure vanilla extract

¼ teaspoon kosher salt

2 tablespoons honey, plus more if desired

1 tablespoon coconut oil

PARFAITS

¼ cup / 45 g amaranth

½ cup / 40 g sliced almonds, toasted (see page 12)

1 teaspoon ground fennel seeds

2 teaspoons unsweetened dark cocoa powder

10 washed ripe fresh figs (about 8.5 ounces / 240 g)

1 tablespoon honey, for serving

To make the Almond Cream: In a bowl, cover the almonds in water and soak at room temperature for 6 hours or overnight. Drain the almonds.

In a blender or food processor fitted with the metal blade, combine the almonds, water, vanilla, salt, honey, and coconut oil. Blend for 2 to 3 minutes at high speed, or until smooth. If the almond cream is still a bit chunky, add 1 to 2 tablespoons more water and continue

continued

blending. It should be smooth yet textured. Taste and add more honey if desired. Cover and refrigerate before using for at least 1 hour or up to 3 days.

❧ To pop the amaranth: Place a small, dry saucepan over high heat and allow it to become quite hot before adding the amaranth. Add the amaranth and shimmy the pan until most of the grains have puffed up or popped and turned white in color, 1 to 2 minutes. Some grains are stubborn and don't necessarily want to pop, but if you have a good mix of puffed and golden amaranth, you're in business. If your amaranth is particularly jumpy, cover with a lid.

❧ To assemble the parfaits: Spoon the popped amaranth into a small bowl. Add the toasted almonds, fennel, and cocoa powder and toss together to combine.

❧ Quarter the figs lengthwise, starting from the stem end. Trim off and discard the stem. For each parfait, layer 3 tablespoons of the almond cream, 4 fig quarters, and 2 tablespoons of the popped amaranth mixture. Repeat the layers once more. Top with two fig quarters and drizzle with the honey.

> **Make Ahead:** *While these parfaits are fine if refrigerated until you're ready to serve them, the amaranth can get soggy after about 30 minutes. For this reason, it's best to assemble them to order. To save time, prepare all of the components of the parfaits (make the almond cream, toast the almonds, pop the amaranth, quarter the figs) and store them separately until ready to assemble (figs and almond cream in the refrigerator, amaranth and almonds covered at room temperature).*

Honeyed Ricotta

This may be my favorite accompaniment in the book. It's wonderful on pretty much everything, especially Buckwheat Crepes (page 118) or Whole-Grain Buttermilk Pancakes (page 36), or stirred into The Very Best Oatmeal (page 30). Ricotta is traditionally made from the whey that's left over from the cheese-making process, and it's often extremely mild. This recipe brightens the simple cheese with a combination of honey, vanilla, and lemon zest—transforming it into a light morning topping that could rival any high-end yogurt or jam. MAKES ABOUT 2 CUPS

15 ounces / 425 g part-skim ricotta

2 tablespoons honey

¼ teaspoon pure vanilla extract

¼ teaspoon grated lemon zest

⇥ In a small bowl, use a whisk to whip all the ingredients together until light and creamy, 1 to 2 minutes. Store in an airtight container in the refrigerator for up to 5 days.

Dark Chocolate Hazelnut Spread

At my farmers' market stand in San Francisco, this recipe was the star. I'd fill homemade toaster tarts with it and sell out each week. When Sam was in town visiting, he'd sneak more than his fair share with coffee in the morning while we waited for the first sleepy customers to stagger by. Today, we make it occasionally to have with whole-grain waffles or the ends of baguettes, or to mix into oatmeal for a treat on the weekends. There are many recipes for chocolate hazelnut spread out there, but I love this one for its simplicity: no melting chocolate, no heating milk, no straining or sifting. While it may seem like a doubtful choice in the quest to eat well in the mornings, this version is comparatively low in sugar and doesn't contain any of the fillers and fluff common in some store-bought brands. MAKES ³/₄ CUP

> **Morning Notes:** *This is the time to use your very best cocoa powder—you'll taste the difference.*

1 cup / 120 g hazelnuts, toasted and skinned (see page 12) and cooled

¹/₄ cup / 25 g unsweetened dark cocoa powder (I use Valrhona)

¹/₂ cup / 50 g confectioners' sugar

³/₄ teaspoon pure vanilla extract

¹/₄ teaspoon kosher salt

2 tablespoons safflower or canola oil

❧ In a food processor fitted with the metal blade, process the hazelnuts until they become a smooth butter, about 3 minutes. Use a wooden spoon to scrape down the sides of the bowl if necessary. Add the cocoa powder, sugar, vanilla, salt, and oil and continue processing until creamy, 1 minute or so. Transfer to an airtight container or your favorite jar. Refrigerated, it will keep for 4 to 6 weeks. If after sitting the spread becomes firmer than you'd like, simply stir in a little more oil, ¹/₂ teaspoon at a time, until the desired consistency. If it remains looser than you'd like, simply stir in more confectioners' sugar, 1 teaspoon at a time.

Spiced Pear Sauce

Come fall, applesauce becomes an instant star in kitchens across the country. But a close cousin, pear sauce spiced with fresh ginger, cinnamon, and a touch of cardamom, is something I find myself really craving when good pears are in season. It's wonderful as is or served on top of Buckwheat Crepes (page 118) or Whole-Grain Buttermilk Pancakes (page 36). It also quickly becomes a star on top of your favorite oatmeal, porridge, or warm grain cereal. MAKES 2½ CUPS

Morning Notes: *I like Bosc or Barlett pears for this recipe. Just know that the cooking time will vary slightly depending on the ripeness of your pears: the firmer they are, the longer they'll take to cook down. In general, the sauce will go from chunky to really juicy, but then it cooks down further to thicken up.*

2 pounds / 900 g ripe pears (4 to 5 large pears), peeled, cored, and diced into 1-inch cubes (about 3 cups / 720 ml)

1 tablespoon grated fresh ginger

1 cinnamon stick

½ teaspoon ground cardamom

¼ cup / 60 ml apple juice or cider

1 teaspoon honey

¼ teaspoon kosher salt

⇥ Combine all the ingredients in a heavy-bottomed saucepan over medium-high heat. Let the mixture come to a boil, then decrease the heat to medium-low. Simmer, stirring occasionally, until the pears are very tender, about 20 minutes. If you like your sauce a little less chunky, mash it with a potato masher or the back of a wooden spoon. Remove and discard the cinnamon stick. Serve warm or scoop into clean glass jars or another airtight container and refrigerate for up to 2 weeks.

Make It Your Own: *For a pop of color and a bit of crunch, I like to add dried cranberries and toasted walnuts. Fold in one (or both) at the very end.*

WINTER
looking ahead

THE RECIPES SAM AND I MAKE IN THE MORNING and the time we spend together around the table—I wouldn't give them up. But at the end of the day, it's a bigger world than our breakfast table, our farmers' market, our Sunday morning. To look beyond ourselves, our table, and our small neighborhood toward the moments when we come together and share meals with friends, share stories with family, set bigger intentions for weeks, months, years—that's the good stuff. These days, that's where I find myself each winter, in a season that, more than any other, begs you to claim it as your own and make of it what you will.

I used to work at a sweet little paper store on Pearl Street in Boulder, Colorado. Every New Year's Day, my boss (and the owner of the shop), Diana, would ride her bike up Four Mile Canyon early in the morning, rain or shine, and set her intentions for the year ahead. At the time, I was a young college student ringing in the occasion with not-so-great beer, and couldn't imagine why anyone would want to spend the day alone in the woods. Now, glad as I am to have Sam and family afoot as the year turns (not to mention much better beer), the celebrations are less the heart of the season. Today the heart of the season is centered more on reflection, creation, and quiet—all perfectly captured in my favorite children's book, Crocket Johnson's *Harold and the Purple Crayon*.

Within these pages, Johnson chronicles the life of a young boy, Harold, and his travels throughout his day. Harold clutches a purple crayon wherever he goes, and when he wants to experience or try something new, he simply draws it and it materializes:

> One evening, after thinking it over for some time, Harold decided to go for a walk in the moonlight. There wasn't any moon and Harold needed a moon for a walk in the moonlight. And he needed something to walk on. He made a long straight path so he wouldn't get lost. And he set off on his walk, taking his big purple crayon with him.

I think Harold would have shared the feeling that winter is ripe—that it practically calls out for, if not demands, reflection and planning. It's a time for consideration, deliberation, and a different sort of building. With that in mind, I try to open my door to it all: a season full of sparkling lights and trails of smoke sneaking out of chimneys, a season of canyons, crayons, and big, expansive intentions. A season meant for creating your own walk, your own path, and maybe even your own moon to light it.

SEASONAL *Spotlight*

Because winter is a dormant season for many fruits and vegetables and a most welcome break for farmers, I tend to become all the more passionate about what the season *does* offer. **Citrus** brings vibrant color and sweetness to winter. In California, bowls of Meyer lemons grace the kitchen table. **Cranberries** are wonderful when you crave a tart hit of flavor. Seek out bright, firm berries and feel free to freeze them for up to 1 year. **Bananas** are ever present and nice to slice into cereals and porridge.

I fold **hearty greens** like kale, mustard greens, and Swiss chard into warm grain bowls, omelets, and frittatas. While it's occasionally thought of as more of a spring green, kale is so prevalent in the winter that I associate it with colder months, too. Lacinato (or dinosaur) kale is a favorite for its flat, broad leaves and mild flavor. **Carrots** are incredible come winter because the cooler temperatures turn their natural starches into sugar, so they're sweet as can be. You can find yellow, purple, and white varieties and use them in everything from soups, stews, and salads to cakes, muffins, and bread. The leafy tops draw moisture out of carrots, so when you refrigerate them, be sure to slice them off; then your carrots will easily keep for a few weeks.

Greens *and* Grains Scramble

This is the breakfast Sam and I probably eat most often regardless of the season. In truth, it's usually a dish we whip up as a late breakfast on weekdays when we're both working from home and most emails have been returned. It's wonderfully versatile and allows you to use up any leftover grains you have from previous meals, folding in leafy greens for a bit of color. In that sense, think of it more as a template rather than a hard-and-fast approach. Any leafy greens and most grains will work, although I veer away from small, delicate grains like amaranth because they can get lost in the dish. SERVES 2, HEARTILY

4 large eggs, beaten

1 tablespoon milk

¼ teaspoon kosher salt

2 tablespoons extra-virgin olive oil

1 green onion, white and light green parts, finely chopped (about 1 tablespoon)

2 cloves garlic, minced

1 heaping cup / 240 ml well-packed chopped leafy greens (such as kale, Swiss chard leaves without ribs, or spinach)

½ cup / 120 ml cooked whole grains (wheat berries, farro, barley, or millet; see pages 22–23)

1 tablespoon chopped fresh chives

Freshly ground black pepper

Flaky salt

Crusty bread, toasted English muffins, or warm corn tortillas, for serving

In a large bowl, whisk together the eggs, milk, and kosher salt; set aside. Heat 1 tablespoon of the olive oil in a sauté pan over medium heat. Add the green onion and garlic and sauté until soft, 1 to 2 minutes. Add the greens, grains, and remaining 1 tablespoon olive oil and sauté until the greens are wilted and the grains are warmed through, 3 to 5 minutes.

Decrease the heat to low and pour in the egg mixture, gently stirring to comingle them with the greens and grains. Continue stirring until they're softly scrambled, 2 to 3 minutes. Remove from the heat, stir in the chives, and season with pepper.

Serve hot with a sprinkling of flaky salt on top, and crusty bread, toasted English muffins, or warm corn tortillas alongside.

Make It Your Own: *Stirring in grated Parmesan cheese or a creamy chèvre is always nice. For a splurge in the late fall or early winter, I can't think of a much better way to begin the morning than cooking up a handful of chanterelles in a bit of butter and folding them into the eggs.*

Spiced Bulgur Porridge *with* Dates, Almonds, *and* Golden Raisins

Sam lived in Poland for almost two years and, true to form, made many new friends—some from the small Mediterranean community in Krakow. In the colder months, they'd often make a creamy porridge served with dates, walnuts, and lots of honey. Today, I make my own version with quick-cooking bulgur wheat and warm spices like cardamom and ginger. If you're making this in the height of fig season, the jammy, sliced fruits are wonderful served on top—as is a sprinkling of date sugar, which can be a bit tough to track down and a little pricey, but it's a wonderful alternative to white sugar. SERVES 4

Morning Notes: *Use a coarser bulgur for a heartier bowl. Medjools are almost always my date of choice as they're easy to find, large, incredibly soft, and supersweet. Look for dates that are plump and dark amber in color. Stored in an airtight container at room temperature, they should stay fresh for 6 to 8 weeks. Alternatively, store in the refrigerator for up to 1 year.*

1 cup / 240 ml water

¼ teaspoon pure vanilla extract

¼ teaspoon ground cinnamon

Pinch of ground cardamom

½ teaspoon kosher salt

¾ cup / 120 g bulgur wheat

1 tablespoon chopped crystallized ginger

1 cup / 240 ml unsweetened almond milk, dairy milk, or soy milk

¾ cup / 120 g pitted and chopped Medjool dates (about 6 large dates)

¼ cup / 35 g golden raisins

¾ cup / 105 g almonds, toasted (see page 12), cooled, and coarsely chopped

⇥ In a medium saucepan, bring the water to a boil. Add the vanilla, cinnamon, cardamom, and salt and stir. Stir in the bulgur and ginger, cover, and remove from the heat. Let stand for 10 minutes, until most of the liquid has absorbed.

⇥ Meanwhile, in a small saucepan, warm the almond milk with the dates and raisins until little bubbles start to form around the rim of the pan. Don't let it come to a full boil. Pour the hot almond milk mixture into the bulgur and cook over medium-low heat, stirring occasionally, until it has a porridge-like consistency, about 7 minutes. I like mine a bit loose and creamy, especially as it tends to thicken a bit once you remove it from the heat.

⇥ Serve warm, topped with toasted almonds. The dish will keep for 3 to 4 days if covered and refrigerated.

HOW TO MAKE BETTER GRANOLA

Dry, tasteless granola is a common affair in the aisles of many grocery stores. This is why I decided to start making my own. Thousands of batches later, I can share a few tips and tricks that I use to help make Marge Granola so wonderfully toasty and flavorful.

1. **You Need Oil:** There's a tendency to want to make granola as healthy as possible, but if you're not using oil (or another fat), you're going to have a pile of dry oats. I use olive oil, but feel free to experiment with coconut oil or a more neutral-flavored oil instead.

2. **Choose Oats Wisely:** You want to use rolled oats, not quick-cooking or instant oats. Quick-cooking oats don't soak up moisture in the same way as rolled oats do, producing an almost dusty, dry granola.

3. **Add Fruit Last:** The best thing about making granola at home is you can add whatever fruits and nuts you like, but you have to consider what to add *before* it bakes and what to add *after*. A general rule of thumb is to add any chopped, dried fruits after the granola comes out of the oven. With Marge Granola, I add coconut flakes about halfway through the baking because they tend to brown quicker than the other ingredients.

4. **Timing Is Everything:** In my experience, granola is like cookies in the sense that it continues baking when you pull it from the oven. As it cools, it firms up a bit, so be sure not to wait until your granola has browned too heavily to pull it out of the oven. Certainly follow the recipe, but do trust your own eyes and intuition, too.

5. **Want Clumpy Granola?** Some folks like to stir an egg white into the wet granola mixture to encourage those sought-after clumps to form. Another trick is not to stir the granola as it's baking, but to rotate the pan to avoid hot spots and burned edges. Then, after cooling, you can remove it from the pan in chunkier pieces.

6. **Mix Dry Ingredients First:** While granola is absolutely a one-bowl affair, you want to mix all of your dry ingredients together before adding your wet ingredients so as to avoid the clumping together of salts and spices which will eventually lead to a very unpleasant bite of granola.

7. **Use Fresh Spices:** The fresher the spices, the better your end product.

8. **Don't Fear Salt!** Salt enhances the flavor of your granola, and most people don't use enough of it. Use it. Really!

9. **Experiment with Savory Additions:** I love using cacao nibs and a little extra salt, which results in an almost savory granola. I've also tried adding dried herbs; rosemary and sage are both delicious.

10. **Use a Firm Press:** When pouring granola onto a baking sheet, make sure the sheet is pretty full (otherwise you'll end up with burned oats), and apply pressure with a spatula to create a nice, flat, uniform layer. This ensures the granola will bake evenly.

Hazelnut Cacao Nib Granola

I'm sure you're familiar with the all-too-good marriage of hazelnuts and chocolate—long a favorite of my sisters and me growing up (we'd often dip spoons and fingers into the Nutella jar, then were always baffled at how it could disappear so quickly). Today, while our tastes have matured, they haven't changed. This is the favorite granola of my youngest sister, Zoe. In the Marge kitchen, I use olive oil, but when I first began experimenting with coconut oil in cookies and cakes, I tried it with this granola recipe and have never turned back. It imparts a subtle sweetness: not edgy or conspicuous, but more of a whisper or a kiss. MAKES 6 TO 7 CUPS

Morning Notes: *I don't bother to skin the hazelnuts for this recipe. For the most part, the skins blend with all the different textures of the granola, and I've never noticed them enough to bother with it.*

3 cups / 300 g rolled oats

½ cup / 60 g raw sesame seeds

½ cup / 50 g raw walnuts, coarsely chopped

1 teaspoon kosher salt

¼ teaspoon ground cinnamon

½ teaspoon ground cardamom

1 teaspoon pure vanilla extract

½ cup / 120 ml maple syrup

½ cup / 120 ml coconut oil, melted

¾ cup / 35 g unsweetened coconut flakes

½ cup / 60 g raw hazelnuts, coarsely chopped

¼ cup / 25 g cacao nibs

⇝ Preheat the oven to 325°F. Line a large rimmed baking sheet with parchment paper or a silicone mat.

⇝ In a large bowl, stir together the oats, sesame seeds, walnuts, salt, cinnamon, and cardamom.

⇝ Add the vanilla, maple syrup, and coconut oil and stir to combine. I use my hands at this point so that all of the wet and dry ingredients are evenly mixed together. Turn the mixture out onto the prepared baking sheet and spread in an even layer.

⇝ Bake for 15 minutes. Remove the baking sheet from the oven and stir in the coconut and hazelnuts. Return to the oven and bake until the granola is fragrant and golden brown, 18 to 20 minutes, stirring once halfway through to ensure that it bakes evenly. Let cool completely. If the granola doesn't seem as toasty as you'd like, much like cookies when they come out of the oven, it will firm up considerably as it cools. Stir in the cacao nibs. Store in an airtight container at room temperature for 3 to 4 weeks or in the refrigerator for up to 6 weeks. The granola also freezes beautifully for up to 3 months.

Trail Guide Nut *and* Seed Bars

In my midtwenties, on a family trip to Banff National Park in Alberta, Canada, I tried cross-country skiing for the first time. I'm not sure if it was the stark, beautiful landscape or the nutty energy bars the trail guides brought along for us, but I fell in love with the sport. Before heading home, I convinced the kitchen staff to give me the recipe, and this is the version that remains after years of tweaks and adaptations. The trick is to let these bars cool completely before you slice them; they firm up considerably as they cool (and note that they take a few hours to cool completely). MAKES 12 TO 15 BARS, DEPENDING ON SIZE

1 tablespoon butter, for greasing the pan

¾ cup / 180 ml brown rice syrup or honey

3 tablespoons maple syrup

¾ cup / 180 ml safflower or canola oil

¾ cup / 180 ml almond butter, homemade (page 163) or store-bought

1 teaspoon pure vanilla extract

3 cups / 300 g rolled oats

¾ cup / 95 g raw pepitas

¼ cup / 30 g raw sunflower seeds

1 cup / 80 g sliced raw almonds

½ cup / 60 g raw cashews, chopped

½ cup / 50 g pecans, coarsely chopped

¼ cup / 30 g raw sesame seeds

¾ cup / 45 g wheat bran or oat bran

½ cup / 60 g dried cranberries

½ cup / 75 g chopped dried apricots

1¼ teaspoons kosher salt

1 teaspoon ground cinnamon

⇢ Preheat the oven to 325°F. Butter a 9 by 13-inch baking pan.

⇢ Mix the brown rice syrup, maple syrup, and oil in a small heavy-bottomed saucepan. Bring to a low simmer over medium-low heat. Remove from the heat, add the almond butter and vanilla, and whisk to combine. Set aside while you prepare the dry ingredients.

⇢ In a very large bowl, mix together the oats, pepitas, sunflower seeds, almonds, cashews, pecans, sesame seeds, bran, dried cranberries, apricots, salt, and cinnamon.

⇢ Pour the warm syrup mixture over the dry ingredients and mix well; I use my hands at this point to make sure everything is fully incorporated. Press the mixture into the prepared pan using the back of a rubber spatula. Bake the bars until the edges are just turning golden brown, 30 to 35 minutes (the bars will still feel a bit soft at this point). Let cool completely in the pan before slicing, about 2 hours.

⇢ Once cool, cut into squares. Wrap the bars in plastic wrap for on-the-go snacking or store, covered, at room temperature for 4 to 5 days.

Make It Your Own: *As long as you keep the amount of dry ingredients the same, feel free to substitute other types of nuts, seeds, and dried fruits, or even little chocolate bits.*

Morning Glory Oats

This recipe takes all of the wonderful flavors of morning glory muffins—those coffee shop favorites studded with raisins, shredded carrots, and coconut—and folds them into a creamy, toothsome porridge. The grated carrots soften into the oats, and the raisins plump and become incredibly sweet. It's filling and nourishing, and it makes me thankful we decided to plant carrots in our small garden out back—now we occasionally have them at the ready to grate into porridge when the craving strikes. SERVES 4

Morning Notes: I make this recipe with part milk and part water, but you could certainly use all water if you'd prefer, or do a straight split of 2 cups water and 2 cups milk.

3 cups / 720 ml water

1 cup / 240 ml milk, plus extra
   for serving

1 cup / 175 g steel-cut oats

1 cup / 100 g grated carrots
   (about 2 medium carrots)

²/₃ cup / 90 g seedless raisins

³/₄ teaspoon ground cinnamon

¹/₄ teaspoon ground ginger

¹/₄ teaspoon ground nutmeg

3 tablespoons light brown sugar

1 teaspoon pure vanilla extract

¹/₂ teaspoon kosher salt

¹/₂ cup / 25 g unsweetened
   coconut flakes

1¹/₂ tablespoons grated orange zest

In a saucepan, bring the water and milk to a gentle boil. Stir in the oats, carrots, raisins, cinnamon, ginger, nutmeg, brown sugar, vanilla, and salt and return to a boil. Decrease the heat to low and partially cover. Cook the porridge without stirring until it begins to thicken and the oats are soft yet chewy, 25 to 30 minutes. Remove from the heat and stir in the coconut flakes and orange zest. Cover and let sit for 5 minutes before serving. Serve warm with an extra glug of warmed milk, if you'd like.

Make Ahead: Refrigerate leftovers in an airtight container and they'll keep for 5 days. Reheat by adding a few tablespoons of additional water or milk and warm on the stovetop or in the microwave, stirring well.

Saucy Tomato Poached Eggs *with* Kale *and* Wheat Berries

I first had shakshuka at Eltana, a wood-fired bagel shop here in Seattle known for their crusty bagels and breads, spreads and schmears, and winter soups. Shakshuka is a traditional Middle Eastern dish of saucy tomatoes, peppers, and runny eggs. When I began writing this book, I couldn't stop thinking about what it would be like if there were hearty whole grains strewn throughout, so my version has chewy wheat berries, along with chopped kale, lemon zest for brightness, and capers for a slightly salty kick. If you're nervous about spice, don't be: the Anaheim peppers are quite flavorful without adding much heat. SERVES 4 TO 6

Morning Notes: *A 12-inch skillet with a lid is ideal to allow all the ingredients to cook evenly and the eggs to poach successfully. Because people are particular about the way they like their eggs, use the timing here as a rough guide but rely on your own best judgment, too. If you're in the mood to experiment with different grains, farro, spelt berries, or rye berries would be great. I'd just avoid any of the tiny grains like amaranth or millet.*

3 tablespoons extra-virgin olive oil, plus more for serving

½ cup / 60 g diced yellow onion (about ½ medium onion)

2 Anaheim chiles, stemmed, seeded, and diced

3 cloves garlic, minced

1 (28-ounce / 800 g) can crushed tomatoes

1 tablespoon tomato paste

¾ cup / 85 g cooked wheat berries (see page 23)

3 tablespoons capers, drained

½ teaspoon ground cumin

1 teaspoon sweet paprika

1 tablespoon grated lemon zest

1 teaspoon kosher salt

½ bunch kale, stemmed and coarsely chopped (about 2½ cups / 125 g)

6 large eggs

¼ cup / 45 g crumbled feta cheese

Flaky salt

Red pepper flakes

⇥ In a 12-inch skillet over medium heat, warm the oil until it shimmers. Add the onion and sauté until just soft, 3 to 4 minutes. Add the chiles and sauté for another 3 to 4 minutes. Then add the garlic and continue sautéing for 1 minute.

⇥ Add the crushed tomatoes, tomato paste, cooked wheat berries, capers, cumin, paprika, lemon zest, and kosher salt and stir well to combine. Simmer, uncovered, over low heat until the sauce starts to thicken, about 15 minutes. Taste and season with more salt as desired.

continued

↝ Fold in the kale and simmer until it begins to soften into the sauce, 1 to 2 minutes. Use a wooden spoon to make 6 little wells in the sauce for the eggs to nestle into. The skillet will be relatively full at this point, so just do your best. Crack the eggs into the wells and cover the skillet. Cook over low heat until the whites are firm but the yolks remain a touch runny, 6 to 8 minutes. Top with the crumbled feta.

↝ Scoop into bowls, sprinkle with flaky salt and red pepper flakes, and drizzle with a dash of olive oil. While I find this best the day it's made, you can allow leftovers to cool completely, then cover with plastic wrap, and refrigerate for up to 2 days.

Pear-Hazelnut Oat Muffins

I don't often bake muffins at home because I find so many of them less than satisfying: a bit too light to get me going in the morning, and often full of white flour and sugar. When I do make muffins, I like them loaded with seasonal fruit and interesting flavors and textures. These fit the bill: they bake up hearty, with shredded pears and chopped hazelnuts folded into a cardamom-scented batter. They make a welcome addition to a fall or winter brunch but are also nice to have around the house on an average weekday when you need something quick to grab in the morning. Baking alert: These muffins look done before they really are. The tops will brown about halfway through their cook-time, but the moist, full-of-fruit centers take a little time to catch up. You'll know they're done when you press gently on the tops and they spring back ever so slightly.

MAKES 12 STANDARD MUFFINS

Morning Notes: *Find the firmest pears possible to avoid mushy pear grating. Bartletts are my usual go-to. Avoid grating the pears until you're ready to put the muffins together or the shredded fruit will brown. And if you'd like to experiment beyond oats, barley or rye flakes are wonderful choices.*

¾ cup / 75 g rolled oats

1 cup / 120 g unbleached all-purpose flour

½ cup / 60 g whole wheat pastry flour

¾ teaspoon baking soda

2 teaspoons baking powder

½ teaspoon ground cardamom

½ teaspoon ground nutmeg

¾ teaspoon kosher salt

2 or 3 firm medium pears

⅔ cup / 125 g natural cane sugar (I use turbinado)

6 tablespoons / 85 g unsalted butter, plus more for greasing the pan

1 cup / 240 ml buttermilk

2 large eggs, beaten

1½ teaspoons pure vanilla extract

1 cup / 120 g hazelnuts, toasted (see page 12), cooled, and coarsely chopped

❧ Preheat the oven to 425°F. Butter a standard 12-cup muffin tin (or line with papers, if you prefer).

❧ In a bowl, combine the oats, flours, baking soda, baking powder, cardamom, nutmeg, and salt. Mix well and set aside.

❧ Peel and core the pears, then grate them into a bowl using the large holes of a box grater. You should end up with about 1 cup / 215 g of shredded pear.

continued

⊰ Put the sugar in a large bowl. In a small saucepan over low heat, melt the butter. Add the butter to the sugar and stir until well combined. Whisk in the buttermilk, eggs, vanilla, and shredded pear until you have what resembles a loose batter. Add the flour mixture and fold it in gently. Reserve ½ cup of the hazelnuts to sprinkle on top of the muffins; stir the other ½ cup into the batter. Be careful not to overmix.

⊰ Fill the muffin cups almost to the top with batter, and sprinkle with the remaining ½ cup of chopped hazelnuts. Put the muffins in the oven and immediately decrease the heat to 375°F. Bake until the tops are golden brown and feel firm to the touch, even in the center, 25 to 27 minutes.

⊰ Let the muffins cool for 10 minutes, then remove from the tin (I use a paring knife to nudge them out). Serve warm or at room temperature. These muffins will keep for 2 days if stored in an airtight container.

Make Ahead: *These muffins freeze well in an airtight container or wrapped individually in plastic wrap. To thaw, leave them out at room temperature for 24 hours or heat in a 200°F oven until warmed through.*

Banana Walnut Baked Oatmeal

I discover recipe ideas from friends, dishes I try at restaurants around town, overheard conversations, and farmers' market strolls. I also get recipe ideas from other cooks and writers. This baked oatmeal is one such case, inspired by Heidi Swanson, creator of the blog *101 Cookbooks*. Heidi developed a recipe for baked oatmeal with huckleberries in her cookbook *Super Natural Every Day*, and for the past year, I've experimented with different ingredients and methods of preparation, finally settling on this version using bananas, walnuts, and ground flaxseeds, and relying on applesauce and maple syrup for natural sweetness. If I had it my way, we'd have a pan of this at the ready throughout the winter.

SERVES 6 TO 8

Morning Notes: *We've made this recipe many times, but one day out of the blue Sam decided to sprinkle a little flaky salt on top of his bowl. It's our new favorite way to serve it: maple syrup, flaky salt, and a splash of warm milk. Because the almonds and walnuts toast in about the same amount of time and it seems fussy to use two separate pans, I toast them together—almonds on one side of the pan, walnuts on the other.*

2 cups / 200 g rolled oats

1/2 cup / 60 g sliced almonds, toasted (see page 12) and cooled

1 cup / 100 g walnuts, toasted (see page 12), cooled, and coarsely chopped

3 tablespoons ground flaxseeds

1 teaspoon baking powder

1 1/4 teaspoons ground cinnamon

1/4 teaspoon ground ginger

1/4 teaspoon ground nutmeg

1 teaspoon kosher salt

1 1/2 cups / 360 ml milk

1/2 cup / 120 ml buttermilk

1/2 cup / 120 ml applesauce

1/3 cup / 80 ml maple syrup, plus more for serving

1 large egg, beaten

1 tablespoon pure vanilla extract

3 ripe bananas cut into 1/2-inch slices (about 1 3/4 cups / 260 g)

3 tablespoons coconut oil or butter, melted, plus more for greasing the pan

Flaky salt (optional)

Warm cream or milk, for serving (optional)

⇥ Preheat the oven to 375°F. Grease an 8-inch square baking dish with a little coconut oil, fully coating the bottom and sides.

⇥ In a large bowl, mix together the oats, almonds, walnuts, flaxseeds, baking powder, cinnamon, ginger, nutmeg, and kosher salt.

In a medium bowl, whisk together 1 cup of the milk and the buttermilk, applesauce, maple syrup, egg, and vanilla. Add to the oat mixture and fold together quickly until just combined. You don't want to stir too vigorously because you'll break up the oats, making them mushy when baked.

In the prepared baking dish, spread an even layer of sliced bananas (this usually takes 2 full bananas). Then evenly spoon half of the oat mixture on top of the bananas. Top with the remaining bananas and then the rest of the oat mixture. Pour the remaining ½ cup milk on top and drizzle with the coconut oil. The mixture will seem really wet at this point. Don't worry; the oats will soak it all up.

Bake until the oatmeal is bubbling and has a slightly golden top, about 40 minutes. Let cool for at least 15 minutes before serving. Serve warm with a drizzle of maple syrup and a sprinkling of flaky salt. Sometimes I like to pour a little warm cream or milk on top when serving. Cover and refrigerate leftovers for 4 to 5 days.

Make It Your Own: Feel free to experiment with different fruits, nuts, and spices that excite you. Pear and cardamom would be delicious, as would apple and hazelnut with a handful of coconut flakes. You can let the seasons guide you, too, adding sliced stone fruit or berries in the summer.

Fried Halloumi *with* Sun-Dried Tomato *and* Roasted Red Pepper Couscous

Sam is Lebanese, so I've gotten used to trips to the Middle Eastern grocery to stock up on good pita, parboiled rice, and grape leaves. As a result, our cupboards are often overflowing with various unique spices and dried grains, making this dish quick and easy to throw together.

If you're not familiar with halloumi, it's a cheese from Cyprus that's made from sheep's and goat's milk. It's firm and a bit salty and really nice for frying because, while soft in texture, it doesn't melt. You can find it at most well-stocked grocery stores. Za'atar is a Middle Eastern spice, fragrant with rich herbs and toasty sesame seeds. While it's widely available in ethnic markets and groceries with big bulk spice sections, I've also included instructions here for a quick version to make at home.

The salty halloumi, sweet roasted peppers, and creamy lemon yogurt sauce create a balanced dish that satisfies that savory midmorning craving with something a little out of the ordinary. It's an obvious choice for cool weather brunches or morning celebrations and is always one of the first dishes to disappear. While not all breakfasts are conversation starters, this one always is. SERVES 4 AS A SIDE PORTION

> **Morning Notes:** *To help you plan ahead, if you pick up one large lemon, its zest and juice will be just enough for this recipe and the Lemony Yogurt Sauce to accompany it.*

COUSCOUS

1 cup plus 2 tablespoons / 270 ml water

1 teaspoon grated lemon zest

1¼ teaspoons ground cinnamon

2 teaspoons ground coriander

3 tablespoons za'atar, homemade (page 159) or store-bought

¾ cup / 110 g whole wheat couscous

¼ cup / 5 g finely chopped fresh flat-leaf parsley

¼ cup / 45 g drained and chopped oil-packed sun-dried tomatoes

¼ cup / 45 g chopped roasted red bell peppers

1 tablespoon extra-virgin olive oil

¾ teaspoon kosher salt

A few grinds of black pepper

continued

FRIED HALLOUMI

1 (8-ounce / 225 g) package halloumi
    cheese

1 tablespoon extra-virgin olive oil,
    plus more for brushing

Juice from ½ lemon

Lemony Yogurt Sauce (page 72)

Za'atar, for serving

⇥ To make the couscous: In a small saucepan bring the water to a boil. Stir in the lemon zest, cinnamon, coriander, za'atar, and couscous. Remove from the heat and let sit, covered, for 10 minutes. Fluff with a fork, then stir in the parsley, sun-dried tomatoes, red peppers, olive oil, salt, and pepper (this recipe goes a bit light on the salt as halloumi is quite salty).

⇥ To fry the halloumi: Unwrap the cheese and blot well with a paper towel to remove some of the moisture. Cut into eight ¼-inch slices (halloumi can break apart easily, so handle it carefully). Warm the olive oil in a large nonstick pan over medium-high heat until hot and shimmering. Lay the slices of cheese in the pan and cook for about 2 minutes. Flip and cook on the second side until browned, an additional 1 to 2 minutes. The cheese should develop a nice, dark brown color on each side. Transfer to a large plate and sprinkle with the lemon juice.

⇥ To assemble: I've served this dish two ways. The first is a bit more casual: I arrange the halloumi slices on a small serving plate nestled up against a mound of the couscous, with the yogurt sauce in a little bowl on the side. Friends help themselves. The second way is more composed and works best if you're doing a plated midmorning meal: I scoop a generous portion of couscous onto each plate, lay 2 slices of grilled halloumi on top, and finish with a dollop of yogurt sauce and a sprinkling of extra za'atar.

Make Ahead: *Make the couscous up to 2 days in advance and store covered in the refrigerator. When you're ready to serve the dish, simply reheat the couscous, fry the halloumi, and assemble. I often double the couscous recipe to have extra for lunch the next day.*

Quick Homemade Za'atar

There are many styles and blends of za'atar. Some go heavy on thyme or coriander while others dip into marjoram. In my experience, it's all about good sumac and sesame seeds, and I tend to favor an equal ratio of thyme and oregano. If you're not familiar with sumac (see Sources, page 166), it has a pretty pronounced lemon flavor, so it's best to balance it with something herbal and earthy. This recipe makes more za'atar than you'll need. Sam uses up any extra by spreading olive oil, bits of garlic, and a generous sprinkling of the herb blend on pita or toasts and baking them until fragrant and crisp. MAKES ABOUT ½ CUP

2 tablespoons dried thyme
2 tablespoons dried oregano
2 tablespoons sesame seeds, lightly toasted (see page 12)
1 tablespoon ground sumac
¼ teaspoon kosher salt

⬧ Place all the ingredients in a spice grinder and pulse several times until you break up the seeds and have a coarse powder (or use a mortar and pestle). Store in an airtight container in the refrigerator, and aim to use within 1 week for the freshest flavor.

Whole-Grain Gingerbread

Gingerbread doesn't have to be relegated to holiday parties or dessert spreads. My version is made with whole-grain flours, tart yogurt, fresh citrus, and a dark spice profile that includes three kinds of ginger. It's a simple, sturdy breakfast, and one that actually gets better the second and third day. For a snowy-topped, celebratory gingerbread, sprinkle with a dusting of confectioners' sugar and serve with a cranberry jam or compote.

SERVES 9 TO 12

> **Morning Notes:** *Spelt flour is a darling in the whole-grain baking world. It acts a lot like all-purpose flour, so it's a great option to pair with a much sturdier flour like whole wheat, adding a bit of lightness to baked goods.*

¾ cup / 120 g whole wheat flour

1 cup / 120 g spelt flour

½ cup / 75 g packed muscovado sugar or brown sugar

¼ teaspoon baking soda

½ teaspoon kosher salt

1 teaspoon ground ginger

¼ cup / 25 g chopped crystallized ginger (optional)

1 tablespoon grated fresh ginger

¼ teaspoon ground cloves

½ teaspoon ground cinnamon

2 tablespoons grated orange zest

¼ teaspoon freshly ground black pepper (optional)

8 tablespoons / 115 g unsalted butter, plus more for greasing the pan

½ cup / 120 ml unsulfured molasses (I use blackstrap)

3 tablespoons honey

½ cup / 120 ml whole milk

¼ cup / 60 ml plain whole-milk yogurt, homemade (page 25) or store-bought

1 large egg, beaten

⇥ Preheat the oven to 350°F. Butter and flour a 9-inch square pan.

⇥ In a large bowl, whisk together the flours, sugar, baking soda, salt, the three kinds of ginger, cloves, cinnamon, orange zest, and pepper. Use your hands to break up any clumps of sugar, and whisk well.

⇥ In a small saucepan over medium-low heat, melt the butter. Add the molasses and honey and cook, stirring, until the mixture is warm but not boiling. Pour into the flour mixture and stir to combine. Add the milk, yogurt, and egg and fold together until combined. With a little arm power, the mixture will soon look like a loose brownie batter.

⇥ Pour the batter into the prepared pan and bake until the edges pull away from the pan slightly and a toothpick inserted into the center comes out clean, 35 to 40 minutes. Let the gingerbread cool completely in the pan before slicing and serving. Any leftovers can be covered and stored at room temperature for up to 4 days.

Savory Barley *with* Mushrooms *and* Parmesan

When I began experimenting with savory oats, I couldn't help but think barley would be pretty wonderful in the mornings, too. Sure enough, this breakfast barley is simple and creamy and makes a satisfying morning meal. Remember that barley is a slow-cooking grain. This recipe takes a good hour to cook fully, but there's something really nice about smelling the developing flavors and knowing you've got a warm, hearty bowl of grains to look forward to. SERVES 4 TO 6

Morning Notes: *If you can, opt for cremini mushrooms here instead of the more common white mushrooms. They're firmer in texture and more complex in flavor, and will hold their shape a little better. And I like low-sodium broth because it affords me more control over seasoning. If you use regular vegetable broth, wait until the very end to add salt.*

2 cups / 480 ml low-sodium
    vegetable broth

2 cups / 480 ml water

1 cup / 200 g pearled barley

2 cups / 120 g thinly sliced cremini
    mushrooms

2 tablespoons fresh thyme

1 teaspoon kosher salt

¼ teaspoon freshly ground black
    pepper

½ cup / 30 g grated Parmesan cheese

2 tablespoons extra-virgin olive oil,
    for serving

Flaky salt

Red pepper flakes (optional)

⇢ In a heavy-bottomed saucepan, bring the broth and water to a low boil over medium heat. Stir in the barley, mushrooms, thyme, kosher salt, and black pepper and return to a low boil. Decrease the heat to low and cover.

⇢ Let the barley cook until most of the liquid is absorbed yet it's still creamy, 60 to 65 minutes. The barley will continue soaking up liquid once it's removed from the heat, so it's okay if it's a little loose when you pull it off the burner.

⇢ Let it sit, covered, off the heat for 10 minutes, then stir in the Parmesan. Taste and season with additional salt and black pepper as desired. Serve hot, drizzled with the olive oil and sprinkled with a bit of flaky salt and red pepper flakes.

Make It Your Own: *If you're not a fan of mushrooms, there are other options. In the fall, fold in small cubes of roasted butternut squash; in the spring, turn to fava beans and thinly-sliced leeks. I especially love this topped with a poached egg (see page 86), regardless of the season.*

Chunky Maple Almond Butter

It's hard to find chunky almond butter in stores, and it's wonderful spread on toast or stirred into your favorite porridge. If you're anything like me, when you make your first batch of almond butter you're going to want to add more oil early in the mixing process, not trusting that it'll actually come together. It will! The almonds release their oils after pulverizing fully. Trust the process, get out some good crusty bread or a crisp apple, and have a seat. MAKES 1¾ CUPS

2⅓ cups / 325 g raw almonds

2 tablespoons safflower or canola oil

2 tablespoons maple syrup

¼ teaspoon pure vanilla extract

½ teaspoon kosher salt

⇁ Put 2 cups of the almonds in the bowl of a food processor fitted with the metal blade and process continuously for 2 minutes. The almonds should look dry and mealy at this point. Add the oil and salt and continue processing for another 8 to 9 minutes, stopping to scrape down the bowl with a wooden spoon every few minutes (avoid a plastic spatula; it can catch on the food processor blade). Be patient here—the nut butter will start out clumpy but will end up smooth if you give it enough time.

⇁ While the mixture is processing, coarsely chop the remaining ⅓ cup almonds and set aside. Add the maple syrup and vanilla to the food processor, and process for another minute or so to combine. You'll notice that the almond butter (and your machine!) will be quite warm at this point—not to worry, both cool quickly. Taste the almond butter and add more salt or maple syrup if you'd like. If you prefer your nut butters a little on the looser side, feel free to add another 1 tablespoon of oil and pulse to combine. Quickly pulse in the chopped almonds, just until incorporated. Transfer to an airtight container. Refrigerate for up to 6 weeks.

Honeyed Tangerine
and Lemon Marmalade

Marmalade can be labor-intensive, with messy time spent removing seeds and pith and hours of overnight resting. This quick version, made with naturally sweet tangerines (or mandarin oranges) and fragrant lemon, is bright and snappy. While I love it on toast, I've also grown quite fond of stirring it into plain yogurt or pairing it with Dark Chocolate Hazelnut Spread (page 133), as well as spreading it on waffles or Whole-Grain Buttermilk Pancakes (page 36). Because it includes honey, this marmalade develops a beautiful dark amber color. MAKES ABOUT 3 CUPS

Morning Notes: *When searching for good tangerines, I like varieties with a tighter rind, like Gold Nugget or Page, but I've also had great luck with the more common varieties of mandarin oranges, like satsumas and clementines. You can use either (although go for seedless to make your life easier). While I'm flexible with varieties of fruit, I do try to buy organic citrus and wash it well since you're using the rind and all—this way, you avoid the chemicals sprayed on many conventional fruits. Last, while I often use natural cane sugar, for this recipe I've had better luck with granulated white sugar; the darker flavors of some natural cane sugars can compete with the flavors of the citrus—which you want to shine.*

1½ pounds / 675 g seedless tangerines
    or mandarin oranges

1 lemon

3 cups / 720 ml water

2 cups / 370 g granulated white sugar

¼ cup / 60 ml honey

⇾ Place a small plate in the freezer to use later for testing the doneness of your marmalade. Wash your jam jars thoroughly and let them dry completely.

⇾ Wash and dry the citrus well. Trim away the ends of the fruit, then slice each into quarters. Remove the seeds from the lemon. Using a sharp knife, slice away the citrus flesh from the peels (some tangerines peel quite easily—lemons are a bit more challenging). Slice the lemon and tangerine peels into thin strips, about ⅛ inch wide (or 1/16 inch wide if you like a more delicate marmalade).

⇾ Fill a pot with water and bring to a boil over high heat. Add the peels only (not the flesh) and let them simmer for just 2 minutes (to help diminish any bitter flavor from the pith). Remove from the heat, drain, and set aside.

⇾ In a large heavy-bottomed pot over high heat, bring the citrus flesh and peels and the water to a boil. Decrease the heat to medium-low and simmer until the citrus peels are tender, 20 to 25 minutes.

✣ Add the sugar and honey and stir well until both dissolve into the mixture. Increase the heat to medium and return to a boil. If there are big segments of citrus that haven't yet cooked down, use a wooden spoon to mash them slightly, creating a more even texture. Cook until the marmalade is reduced by half, begins to thicken, and turns an amber color, 35 to 40 minutes (see note, following, on how to gauge doneness). Stir occasionally to ensure it isn't sticking to the pan. Remove from the heat and pour into the prepared glass jars or heatproof airtight containers. Let the marmalade cool completely, uncovered. Cover and store in the refrigerator for up to 3 weeks or in the freezer for up to 6 months.

How to Tell If It's Done: *To test the marmalade for doneness, place a small dab on a plate that's been chilled in the freezer and freeze for 2 minutes. It is done if a thin film develops on the surface and the marmalade stiffens to appear more jammy than liquid-y. If it simply spreads out and thins, it's not done and needs further cooking.*

SOURCES

While a great deal of the grains, spices, and fresh ingredients I buy for day-to-day cooking are either from the farmers' market or the bulk bins at the grocery store, there are a variety of producers that I seek out specifically or order from online. Here are a few of my favorites.

Anson Mills

www.ansonmills.com

Anson Mills takes their heirloom stone-ground cornmeal and polenta pretty seriously. You can buy different grinds and varieties (such as blue, white, or yellow cornmeal), and you'll notice a difference in taste right away. Other specialties include a wide range of heirloom grains, rice, and incredibly tasty Sea Island peas.

Bluebird Grains

www.bluebirdgrainfarms.com

The best farro and wheat berries I've ever had come from Washington-based Bluebird Grains. They specialize in 100-percent organic grains, flours, and cereal blends, harvested and milled to order.

Bob's Red Mill

www.bobsredmill.com

I use Bob's Red Mill products more than any other. They're my go-to for steel-cut oats, millet, millet grits, quinoa, everyday cornmeal (Anson Mills is my splurge cornmeal), and a few types of whole-grain flours (spelt in particular). Widely available in many grocery stores, with an even wider selection online.

Deluxe Jam

www.deluxe-foods.com

I couldn't choose just one jam purveyor to include here. I have two favorites, fittingly one from California and one from Seattle. My friend Rebecca, in Seattle, makes a mean Pear Butter with Vanilla and a Gingered Rhubarb Jam I'd walk miles for. Both are wonderful spooned on top of porridge or pancakes.

Freddy Guys

www.freddyguys.com

A small family-run Oregon farm that grows and roasts their own hazelnuts. The nuts arrive at your doorstep with the skins partially removed—a huge time-saver in the kitchen.

Inna Jams

www.innajam.com

My friend Dafna is behind Inna Jam in the Bay Area. Her Polka Raspberry and Blenheim Apricot are to die for—they're my favorite slather-on-toast jams and also make wonderful fillings for crepes.

King Arthur Flour

www.kingarthurflour.com

King Arthur is a great resource for whole-grain flours and all sorts of home baking ingredients and equipment. Their website tells you the protein content of each flour and how to get started with them, and even gives relevant recipes. I use their standard whole wheat and whole wheat pastry flour exclusively and have been known to add candied citrus or diced ginger to my order.

Massa Organics

www.massaorganics.com

A fourth-generation California rice farm, Massa Organics produces some of the best whole-grain brown rice I've ever had. I discovered them at a farmers' market in San Francisco and fell in love with their rice immediately. It's nuttier and even a touch sweet. You can find it at select grocery stores or order directly from them online.

The Meadows

www.atthemeadow.com

The Meadows, with locations in Portland and New York City, is one of my favorite spots to pop in for gourmet salts, chocolates, or bitters. I use their flaky salts for finishing recipes in this book.

Mountain Rose Herbs

www.mountainroseherbs.com

If you have trouble finding little muslin bags for making infused honeys, this is a good, affordable online source. Also check out their impressive tea selection (you can grab chamomile flowers here), seasoning blends, and sprouting seeds.

New England Cheesemaking Supply Company

www.cheesemaking.com

From sweet and light to creamy and tangy, you can start to experiment with homemade yogurt using wonderful powdered starters from this company. You can also pick up a few pieces of cheesecloth while you're at it.

Nuts.com

www.nuts.com

Supplier of conventional and organic nuts, seeds, dried fruits, and more. When I'm experimenting with new granola or muesli flavors and want to try, say, dried raspberries or goji berries, they are always a great, friendly resource. I've ordered dried apricots for Marge Granola from them, too.

Penzeys Spices

www.penzeys.com

For whole or ground spices (including sumac), herbs, blends, and extracts that reach beyond the corner grocery store, Penzeys has rarely failed me. High-quality and generally affordable.

Spectrum Organics

www.spectrumorganics.com

A good source for organic, unrefined canola and safflower oils. I also buy their flaxseeds.

Stannard Farm

www.stannardfarm.com

This small Vermont farm supplies the organic maple syrup I use for Marge Granola.

Theo Chocolate

www.theochocolate.com

Seattle is home to the Theo Chocolate Factory, specializing in organic and fair-trade chocolates. While I fell in love with their bars to buy as gifts (or to stow a few away at home), I love their cacao nibs and use them in Marge Granola.

Valrhona

www.valrhona-chocolate.com

For dark cocoa powder, Valrhona isn't the cheapest, but I think it's the best. I use it in my Dark Chocolate Hazelnut Spread (page 133).

Weck Jars

www.weckjars.com

While I don't do much canning, I do store all of my grains and flours in glass jars, and I've been known to do a lot of quick jams in the spring and summer. Mason jars are in heavy rotation, but so are the smartly designed, handsome German Weck jars.

Whole Grains Council

www.wholegrainscouncil.org

This is the source for reliable information on everything pertaining to whole grains, from nutritional information to inspired recipes, news, and health studies. Their "Whole Grains 101" section is a great starting point for anyone wanting to learn more about incorporating whole grains into their diet.

Wholesome Sweeteners

www.wholesomesweeteners.com

A great source for natural cane sugars or molasses. They also carry Billington's delicious, moist muscovado sugar.

Your Local Farmers' Market

www.localharvest.org

A great resource to learn more about farmers' markets, farms, CSAs, and co-ops in your area.

ACKNOWLEDGMENTS

This cookbook wouldn't have come together without the help and support of many close friends, family, and colleagues. I hope all of you know that my door is always open should you land in Seattle; I'd love to make you breakfast.

To my mom, a tireless cheerleader of everything I pursue. For teaching us the importance of gathering around the table, buying yourself fresh flowers, and reading what excites you.

To my dad for early childhood waffles and breakfasts out at Betty Mae's. For showing me what it looks like to start and grow your own business with style and grace, and to do it your own way. Marge wouldn't be what it is without you.

To my Grandma Estelle for sending me poetry in the mail, making killer guacamole, and encouraging me to take risks.

To friends and colleagues who helped along the way: Shauna James Ahern for constant encouragement, killer quinoa (thanks, Danny!), and help realizing the best organization for this book. Tara Austen Weaver for innumerable strolls around the lake. Heidi Swanson for assuring me I could, in fact, do it. Emma Christensen and Sara Renee Forte for moral support—even late at night.

To my agent, Jenni Ferrari-Adler, the quickest email responder on this planet, for reaching out and beginning a conversation that has developed into a wonderful working relationship that I'm ever grateful for. To my publisher, Ten Speed Press, for believing in the project from the beginning. To my editor, Sara Golski, for gently guiding this book into a tighter form. To designer extraordinaire Sarah Adelman for laying out the pages and cover design of this book in a way that feels truly like "me."

To my photographer, Clare Barboza, who understood my aesthetic vision right away, and to superstar food stylist Julie Hopper for making my pear muffins look better than they ever do in my own kitchen. To Betsy Stromberg for her keen eye and art direction. To Kip Beelman for helping me through occasional Lightroom panic attacks.

To my incredible cast and crew of recipe testers: I know that grocery shopping for ingredients and fitting a recipe into your day is no easy thing, and you all have my immense gratitude. This book wouldn't be nearly as good without you: Stephen and Chris Gordon, Rachael and Zoe Gordon, Dana Wooten, Mike Schultz, Chaz Voorhis, Ryan Swanson, Carol Painter, Ashley Rodriquez, Shauna James Ahern, Amy Palanjian, and Tara O'Brady.

To the readers of *A Sweet Spoonful* for continuing to show up each week.

And last, to my Sam: my biggest support, most enthusiastic taste tester, and in-home bartender. You are the reason I moved to Seattle and the reason this book exists in the way that it does. I can't imagine anyone else I'd rather share breakfast with, and I look forward to waking up to each and every one with you.

BIBLIOGRAPHY

I love looking at the back of cookbooks to see what sources informed or inspired a cook I admire. Below you'll find a handful of books that I used as references or resources during the journey of writing this book. I'm grateful to all of the authors for their insight, intelligence, and inspiration.

Bittman, Mark. *How to Cook Everything*. New York: Wiley, 1998.

Boyce, Kim. *Good to the Grain*. New York: Stuart, Tabori and Chang, 2010.

Chernila, Alana. *The Homemade Pantry*. New York: Clarkson Potter, 2012.

Clark, Melissa. *Cook This Now*. New York: Hyperion, 2011.

Dahl, Sophie. *Very Fond of Food*. Berkeley: Ten Speed Press, 2011.

Finlayson, Judith. *The Complete Whole Grains Cookbook*. Toronto: Robert Rose, 2008.

Greene, Bert. *The Grains Cookbook*. New York: Workman Publishing, 1988.

Herbst, Sharon Tyler. *The New Food Lover's Companion*. Hauppage, NY: Barron's Educational Series, Inc. 2001.

Madison, Deborah. *Vegetable Literacy*. Berkeley: Ten Speed Press, 2013.

Page, Karen, and Andrew Dornenburg. *The Flavor Bible*. New York: Little, Brown and Company, 2008.

Pennington, Amy. *The Urban Pantry*. Seattle: Skipstone, 2010.

Sass, Lorna. *Whole Grains Every Day, Every Way*. New York: Clarkson Potter, 2006.

———. *Whole Grains for Busy People*. New York: Clarkson Potter, 2008.

Speck, Maria. *Ancient Grains for Modern Meals*. Berkeley: Ten Speed Press, 2011.

Swanson, Heidi. *Super Natural Every Day*. Berkeley: Ten Speed Press, 2011.

Weil, Andrew, and Rosie Daley. *The Healthy Kitchen*. New York: Knopf, 2003.

Whole Living Magazine editors. *Power Foods*. New York: Clarkson Potter, 2010.

Wizenberg, Molly. *A Homemade Life*. New York: Simon and Schuster, 2009.

ABOUT THE AUTHOR

MEGAN GORDON is a writer, recipe developer, and culinary educator living in Seattle. She writes regularly for The Kitchn and on her blog *A Sweet Spoonful*. Her work has appeared in numerous national magazines including *Better Homes and Gardens*, *Ready Made Magazine* and the Edible publications. When not writing about food, Megan teaches cooking classes and bakes/operates her artisan granola company, Marge, which is distributed nationally and has been recognized by *The Wall Street Journal* and *Sunset* magazine. Megan lives in a little blue Craftsman house with her partner, Sam. Visit her blog at asweetspoonful.com.

INDEX

Saucy Tomato Poached Eggs with Kale and
Wheat Berries, 148–50
Zucchini Farro Cakes Topped with a Quick
Fried Egg, 88
Equipment, 13–14

F

Farro, 19–20, 23
Greens and Grains Scramble, 140
Oven-Baked Asparagus, Pea, and Farro
Frittata, 58–59
Warm Farro Breakfast Bowl with Apples,
Cranberries, and Hazelnuts, 109
Zucchini Farro Cakes, Two Ways, 87–88
Figs, 105
Creamy Breakfast Rice with Honey-Poached
Figs and Pistachios, 114–15
Fresh Fig Parfaits with Popped Amaranth
and Almond Cream, 128–30
Flaxseeds
Banana Walnut Baked Oatmeal, 154–55
Dried Cherry, Almond, and Flax Muesli, 82
Flours, whole-grain, 12–13. See also *individual
flours*
Frittata, Oven-Baked Asparagus, Pea,
and Farro, 58–59
Fruits
Fruit-on-the-Bottom Yogurt, 26
local, 7
Make-Your-Own Signature Granola, 34
organic, 7
See also *individual fruits*

G

Gingerbread, Whole-Grain, 160
Grains, whole
benefits of, 15
buying, 15
cooking, 3–4, 20–23
definition of, 15
flours, 12–13
freezing, 16
gluten-free, 17, 18, 19, 20
leftover cooked, 16–17
rinsing, 16
rolled, 16–17
soaking, 16, 83

storing, 15–16
toasting, 21
See also *individual grains*
Granola
Apricot Pistachio Granola, 57
Hazelnut Cacao Nib Granola, 145
Make-Your-Own Signature Granola, 34
Marge Granola, 33, 69, 144
tips for making, 144
Greens, 139
Greens and Grains Scramble, 140
See also Kale
Grits. See Cornmeal, polenta, and grits

H

Ham
Rocky Mountain Couscous, 55
Hash, Red Flannel Buckwheat, 116–17
Hasty Pudding with Golden Raisins and
Pepitas, 110
Hazelnuts
Baked Pumpkin Risotto, 121–23
Cherry Hazelnut Quinoa Bars, 52
Chocolate Hazelnut Milk, 38
Dark Chocolate Hazelnut Spread, 133
Hazelnut Cacao Nib Granola, 145
Hazelnut Milk, 38
Pear-Hazelnut Oat Muffins, 151–53
toasting, 12
Warm Farro Breakfast Bowl with Apples,
Cranberries, and Hazelnuts, 109
Herbs
fresh vs. dried, 8
Green Herb Sauce, 73
Herbed Goat Cheese, 88
Honey, 9–10
Chai-Spiced Honey, 42
Chamomile Honey, 40
Honeyed Ricotta, 131
Honeyed Tangerine and Lemon
Marmalade, 164–65
Triple-Citrus Honey, 42
Vanilla Bean Honey, 41
Huckleberries, 105
Huckleberry Cornmeal Custard, 124–25

J

Jam, Strawberry Rhubarb Quick, 71

MEASUREMENT CONVERSION CHARTS

VOLUME

U.S.	IMPERIAL	METRIC
1 tablespoon	½ fl oz	15 ml
2 tablespoons	1 fl oz	30 ml
¼ cup	2 fl oz	60 ml
⅓ cup	3 fl oz	90 ml
½ cup	4 fl oz	120 ml
⅔ cup	5 fl oz (¼ pint)	150 ml
¾ cup	6 fl oz	180 ml
1 cup	8 fl oz (⅓ pint)	240 ml
1¼ cups	10 fl oz (½ pint)	300 ml
2 cups (1 pint)	16 fl oz (⅔ pint)	480 ml
2½ cups	20 fl oz (1 pint)	600 ml
1 quart	32 fl oz (1⅔ pints)	1 L

TEMPERATURE

FAHRENHEIT	CELSIUS/GAS MARK
250°F	120°C/gas mark ½
275°F	135°C/gas mark 1
300°F	150°C/gas mark 2
325°F	160°C/gas mark 3
350°F	175 or 180°C/gas mark 4
375°F	190°C/gas mark 5
400°F	200°C/gas mark 6
425°F	220°C/gas mark 7
450°F	230°C/gas mark 8
475°F	245°C/gas mark 9
500°F	260°C

LENGTH

U.S.	METRIC
¼ inch	6 mm
½ inch	1.25 cm
¾ inch	2 cm
1 inch	2.5 cm
6 inches (½ foot)	15 cm
12 inches (1 foot)	30 cm

WEIGHT

U.S./IMPERIAL	METRIC
½ oz	15 g
1 oz	30 g
2 oz	60 g
¼ lb	115 g
⅓ lb	150 g
½ lb	225 g
¾ lb	350 g
1 lb	450 g